Presented to

_____

By

_____

On the Occasion of

_____

Date

_____

THE BIBLE
PROMISE BOOK
for Nurses

COMPILED BY
CATHY MARIE HAKE, R.N.
AND
DEBORAH BOONE

BARBOUR
PUBLISHING

Cover image © Photonica

Published by Barbour Publishing, Inc., P.O. Box 719, Uhrichsville, Ohio 44683
www.barbourbooks.com

Our mission is to publish and distribute inspirational products offering exceptional value and biblical encouragement to the masses.

Member of the
Evangelical Christian
Publishers Association

Printed in China.
5 4 3 2 1

INTRODUCTION

The 23rd Psalm

The LORD is my shepherd; I shall not want. He maketh me to lie down in green pastures: he leadeth me beside the still waters. He restoreth my soul: he leadeth me in the paths of righteousness for his name's sake. Yea, though I walk through the valley of the shadow of death, I will fear no evil: for thou art with me; thy rod and thy staff they comfort me. Thou preparest a table before me in the presence of mine enemies: thou anointest my head with oil; my cup runneth over. Surely goodness and mercy shall follow me all the days of my life: and I will dwell in the house of the LORD for ever.

CONTENTS

I believe the two most serious impediments to recovery from any addictive process are pride and fear. If people can admit powerlessness and initially seek somebody or something greater than themselves, and work the steps, they can and will recover. That is how I personally started, but today the greatest gift of my addiction has been a developing relationship of love and trust in Jesus Christ, the God of my understanding.

MOLLY TUTON, RN, CDNS

Therefore if any man be in Christ, he is a new creature: old things are passed away; behold, all things are become new.　　2 CORINTHIANS 5:17

My son, if sinners entice thee, consent thou not.
PROVERBS 1:10

A new heart also will I give you, and a new spirit will I put within you: and I will take away the stony heart out of your flesh, and I will give you an heart of flesh.   EZEKIEL 36:26

Brethren, if a man be overtaken in a fault, ye which are spiritual, restore such an one in the spirit of meekness; considering thyself, lest thou also be tempted.   GALATIANS 6:1

Fools think they are doing right,

but the wise listen to advice.

PROVERBS 12:15 NCV

Woe unto them that rise up early in the morning, that they may follow strong drink; that continue until night, till wine inflame them!   ISAIAH 5:11

Ointment and perfume rejoice the heart: so doth the sweetness of a man's friend by hearty counsel.
                    PROVERBS 27:9

Give instruction to a wise man, and he will be yet wiser: teach a just man, and he will increase in learning.   PROVERBS 9:9

A fool despiseth his father's instruction: but he that regardeth reproof is prudent.   PROVERBS 15:5

Let your moderation be known unto all men. The Lord is at hand.   PHILIPPIANS 4:5

For the drunkard and the glutton shall come to poverty: and drowsiness shall clothe a man with rags.   PROVERBS 23:21

Wine is a mocker, strong drink is raging: and whosoever is deceived thereby is not wise.

PROVERBS 20:1

Now therefore beware, I pray thee, and drink not wine nor strong drink, and eat not any unclean thing.   JUDGES 13:4

Lord, you know the frailty of man. You alone know when I stumble and fall. Lord, help me in my weakness. Shelter me in your loving-kindness. I acknowledge that only in Your strength can I be whole, for when I am weak, You are strong. Teach me to look to You for my daily sustenance. Grant me wisdom to make choices that are pleasing to You. Teach me to reach out and help others as they reach out to help me. Amen.

ADVERSITY

All adversity is temporary. Time proves that out. God can't be anything but faithful, because that is His nature. What we have to do is keep our eyes focused on Him; the adversity—whatever it is—pales in comparison.

CAROLYN KANOW, RN

Though I walk in the midst of trouble, thou wilt revive me: thou shalt stretch forth thine hand against the wrath of mine enemies, and thy right hand shall save me.

PSALM 138:7

These things I have spoken unto you, that in me ye might have peace. In the world ye shall have tribulation: but be of good cheer; I have overcome the world.

JOHN 16:33

God is our refuge and strength, a very present help in trouble. Therefore will not we fear, though the earth be removed, and though the mountains be carried into the midst of the sea; though the waters thereof roar and be troubled, though the mountains shake with the swelling thereof.   PSALM 46:1–3

For I reckon that the sufferings of this present time are not worthy to be compared with the glory which shall be revealed in us.   ROMANS 8:18

If we suffer,

we shall also reign with him.

2 TIMOTHY 2:12

Beloved, think it not strange concerning the fiery trial which is to try you, as though some strange thing happened unto you: But rejoice, inasmuch as ye are partakers of Christ's sufferings; that, when his glory shall be revealed, ye may be glad also with exceeding joy.   1 PETER 4:12–13

But the God of all grace, who hath called us unto his eternal glory by Christ Jesus, after that ye have suffered a while, make you perfect, stablish, strengthen, settle you.   1 PETER 5:10

13

That the trial of your faith, being much more precious than of gold that perisheth, though it be tried with fire, might be found unto praise and honour and glory at the appearing of Jesus Christ.

1 PETER 1:7

For our light affliction, which is but for a moment, worketh for us a far more exceeding and eternal weight of glory.   2 CORINTHIANS 4:17

The righteous cry, and the LORD heareth, and delivereth them out of all their troubles.

PSALM 34:17

For as the sufferings of Christ abound in us, so our consolation also aboundeth by Christ. And whether we be afflicted, it is for your consolation and salvation, which is effectual in the enduring of the same sufferings which we also suffer: or whether we be comforted, it is for your consolation and salvation.

2 CORINTHIANS 1:5–6

Dear Lord, there is no trouble that has come to man that You have not seen. Give me Your strength to rest in; restore to me the joy of Your salvation so that I shall walk uprightly before You. Teach me, guide me, lead me, so that I might be a witness to others of Your wondrous love and mercy. Amen.

I come to present the strong claims of suffering humanity. I come to place before the Legislature of Massachusetts the condition of the miserable, the desolate, the outcast. I come as the advocate of helpless, forgotten, insane men and women; of beings sunk to a condition from which the unconcerned world would start with real horror.

DOROTHEA DIX,
MEMORIAL TO THE LEGISLATURE OF
MASSACHUSETTS, 1843

And he said unto me, My grace is sufficient for thee: for my strength is made perfect in weakness.
2 CORINTHIANS 12:9

Now we exhort you. . .comfort the feebleminded, support the weak, be patient toward all men.
1 THESSALONIANS 5:14

Here's an incredible word picture of descent into Alzheimer's/dementia from the psalmist:

O LORD God of my salvation, I have cried day and night before thee: let my prayer come before thee: incline thine ear unto my cry; for my soul is full of troubles: and my life draweth nigh unto the grave. I am counted with them that go down into the pit: I am as a man that hath no strength. . . . Thou hast laid me in the lowest pit, in darkness, in the deeps. . . . Thou hast put away mine acquaintance far from me; thou hast made me an abomination unto them: I am shut up, and I cannot come forth. . . . LORD, I have called daily upon thee, I have stretched out my hands unto thee. . . . Shall thy wonders be known in the dark? and thy righteousness in the land of forgetfulness? . . . LORD, why castest thou off my soul? why hidest thou thy face from me? I am afflicted and ready to die from my youth up: while I suffer thy terrors I am distracted. . . . They came round about me daily like water; they compassed me about together. Lover and friend hast thou put far from me, and mine acquaintance into darkness.

PSALM 88:1–4, 6, 8–9, 12, 14–15, 17–18

I have shewed you all things, how that so labouring ye ought to support the weak, and to remember the words of the Lord Jesus, how he said, It is more blessed to give than to receive.		ACTS 20:35

Hearken unto thy father

that begat thee,

and despise not thy mother

when she is old.

PROVERBS 23:22

Gentle Shepherd, I usually think of the lost lamb You sought as being one who strayed away in sin. You'd be every bit as tender with this lost lamb—the one who wants to wander off, who can't care for himself. He's no longer himself—confused, angry, combative, muddled, difficult. He takes so much time and patience, and I have so little of both. Heavenly Father, help me to understand the helplessness and frailty of the wandering mind. Let me lean on Your shepherd's staff and tend this lamb of Yours in Your name, for his comfort and Your glory. Allow me to encourage those who are faced each day with the diminishing capacity of the one they love. Amen.

ANGER

*A nger is normal. It's how we deal with it that makes the
difference. Because of our Christian beliefs, we don't
direct it inward or spill it onto those for whom we care. We
turn it over to God.*

DOTTIE CRUMMY, PH.D., CHAIR, DEPARTMENT OF
NURSING, POINT LOMA NAZARENE UNIVERSITY

The LORD is gracious, and full of compassion; slow
to anger, and of great mercy.   PSALM 145:8

Make no friendship with an angry man; and with a
furious man thou shalt not go: lest thou learn his
ways, and get a snare to thy soul. PROVERBS 22:24–25

He that is slow to anger is better than the mighty;
and he that ruleth his spirit than he that taketh a
city.   PROVERBS 16:32

My dear brothers, take note of this: Everyone should be quick to listen, slow to speak and slow to become angry, for man's anger does not bring about the righteous life that God desires.

James 1:19–20 niv

Be not hasty in thy spirit to be angry: for anger resteth in the bosom of fools.   Ecclesiastes 7:9

A quick-tempered man does foolish things.

Proverbs 14:17 niv

The discretion of a man deferreth his anger; and it is his glory to pass over a transgression.

Proverbs 19:11

Let all bitterness, and wrath, and anger, and clamour, and evil speaking, be put away from you, with all malice.   Ephesians 4:31

A wrathful man stirreth up strife: but he that is slow to anger appeaseth strife.   Proverbs 15:18

Refrain from anger and turn from wrath; do not fret—it leads only to evil.   Psalm 37:8 niv

A soft answer turneth away wrath: but grievous words stir up anger.   Proverbs 15:1

Be ye angry, and sin not: let not the sun go down upon your wrath.   Ephesians 4:26

An angry man stirreth up strife, and a furious man aboundeth in transgression.   PROVERBS 29:22

A wise man fears the LORD and shuns evil, but a fool is hotheaded and reckless.   PROVERBS 14:16 NIV

Do all things without

murmurings and disputings.

PHILIPPIANS 2:14

But now ye also put off all these; anger, wrath, malice, blasphemy, filthy communication out of your mouth.   COLOSSIANS 3:8

He that is slow to wrath is of great understanding: but he that is hasty of spirit exalteth folly.

PROVERBS 14:29

Almighty Lord, sometimes it is so tempting to let my emotions carry me away. Grant me the strength to be a warrior when it is in Your plan, but give me the humility to release what hurts my pride and the love to forgive in Your name. Amen.

A s we seek assurance and God's protection, the concepts of belief, trust, and expectation come to mind. An image of God walking in front of me, beside me, and behind me. . .gives a sense of peace and security only God can provide. A prayer for God's protection throughout the day can bring peace and security if we believe, trust, and expect God to provide that protection step-by-step and day by day.

MARGARET K. JORDAN, RN, MSN,
STUDENT CHRISTIAN NURSE FELLOWSHIP ADVISOR
ASSISTANT PROFESSOR, TEXAS A&M UNIVERSITY,
CORPUS CHRISTI

For God so loved the world, that he gave his only begotten Son, that whosoever believeth in him should not perish, but have everlasting life.

JOHN 3:16

For the wages of sin is death; but the gift of God is eternal life through Jesus Christ our Lord.

ROMANS 6:23

If we confess our sins, he is faithful and just to forgive us our sins, and to cleanse us from all unrighteousness.

1 JOHN 1:9

Verily, verily,

I say unto you,

He that believeth on me

hath everlasting life.

JOHN 6:47

And they said, Believe on the Lord Jesus Christ, and thou shalt be saved, and thy house.

ACTS 16:31

He that believeth on the Son hath everlasting life: and he that believeth not the Son shall not see life; but the wrath of God abideth on him.

JOHN 3:36

But as many as received him, to them gave he power to become the sons of God, even to them that believe on his name.

JOHN 1:12

That if thou shalt confess with thy mouth the Lord Jesus, and shalt believe in thine heart that God hath raised him from the dead, thou shalt be saved.   ROMANS 10:9

For whosoever shall call upon the name of the Lord shall be saved.   ROMANS 10:13

I am come a light into the world, that whosoever believeth on me should not abide in darkness.

JOHN 12:46

And Jesus said unto them, I am the bread of life: he that cometh to me shall never hunger; and he that believeth on me shall never thirst.   JOHN 6:35

Jesus said unto him, If thou canst believe, all things are possible to him that believeth.   MARK 9:23

Heavenly Father, I am awed by the boundless grace and endless love You have given to me. As the psalmist said, "When I consider thy heavens, the work of thy fingers, the moon and the stars, which thou hast ordained; what is man that thou art mindful of him?" And yet, Father, You show us in Your Word, and by the gift of Your precious Son, how very much we mean to You. I offer the humblest of thanks for the incredible gift of Your salvation. Amen.

COMFORT

O *ne of the essential qualities of the clinician is interest in humanity, for the secret of the care of the patient is in caring for the patient.*

FRANCES WELD PEABODY,
in *The Care of the Patient*

Cast thy burden upon the LORD, and he shall sustain thee: he shall never suffer the righteous to be moved. PSALM 55:22

Blessed be God, even the Father of our Lord Jesus Christ, the Father of mercies, and the God of all comfort; who comforteth us in all our tribulation, that we may be able to comfort them which are in any trouble, by the comfort wherewith we ourselves are comforted of God. For as the sufferings of Christ abound in us, so our consolation also aboundeth by Christ. 2 CORINTHIANS 1:3–5

I will not leave you comfortless: I will come to you.
JOHN 14:18

For the LORD will not cast off for ever: But though he cause grief, yet will he have compassion according to the multitude of his mercies. For he doth not afflict willingly nor grieve the children of men.
LAMENTATIONS 3:31–33

As one whom his mother comforteth, so will I comfort you.
ISAIAH 66:13

Comfort ye, comfort ye my people, saith your God.
ISAIAH 40:1

Be perfect, be of good comfort, be of one mind, live in peace; and the God of love and peace shall be with you.
2 CORINTHIANS 13:11

For he hath not despised nor abhorred the affliction of the afflicted; neither hath he hid his face from him; but when he cried unto him, he heard.
PSALM 22:24

Though he fall, he shall not be utterly cast down: for the LORD upholdeth him with his hand.
PSALM 37:24

But the salvation of the righteous is of the LORD: he is their strength in the time of trouble.
PSALM 37:39

And, lo, I am with you always, even unto the end of the world. Matthew 28:20

Come unto me, all ye that labour and are heavy laden, and I will give you rest. Matthew 11:28

The LORD also will be a refuge for the oppressed, a refuge in times of trouble. Psalm 9:9

Come near to God and he will come near to you.

James 4:8 NIV

And I will pray the Father, and he shall give you another Comforter, that he may abide with you for ever. John 14:16

Father, I am so glad I can come to You when I need comfort. There is nothing I face that You haven't seen, no hurt that You don't understand. I know You care, that You are there to lend me the strength I need to go on. Lord, thank You for Your precious sustenance when I am in need of Your tender touch. Thank You for Your unfailing faithfulness. Amen.

It is not how much we do, but how much love we put in the doing. It is not how much we give, but how much love we put in the giving.

MOTHER TERESA

And ye shall eat in plenty, and be satisfied, and praise the name of the LORD your God, that hath dealt wondrously with you: and my people shall never be ashamed.   JOEL 2:26

O give thanks unto the LORD; for he is good: for his mercy endureth for ever.   PSALM 136:1

It is a good thing to give thanks unto the LORD, and to sing praises unto thy name, O most High: to shew forth thy lovingkindness in the morning, and thy faithfulness every night.   PSALM 92:1–2

And my people shall be satisfied with my goodness, saith the LORD.   JEREMIAH 31:14

Let your conversation be without covetousness; and be content with such things as ye have: for he hath said, I will never leave thee, nor forsake thee.
HEBREWS 13:5

You open your hand and satisfy the desires of every living thing.   PSALM 145:16 NIV

In every thing give thanks:
for this is the will of God
in Christ Jesus concerning you.

1 THESSALONIANS 5:18

But godliness with contentment is great gain.
1 TIMOTHY 6:6

My soul, wait thou only upon God; for my expectation is from him.   PSALM 62:5

Keep thy heart with all diligence; for out of it are the issues of life.   PROVERBS 4:23

Be careful for nothing; but in every thing by prayer and supplication with thanksgiving let your requests be made known unto God. And the peace of God, which passeth all understanding, shall keep your hearts and minds through Christ Jesus.

PHILIPPIANS 4:6–7

Gracious Father, I give thanks to You for all You have done for me, for all You have given me. My life is so full, and the riches are all from Your storehouse. The contentment I feel is all due to Your presence in my life. Each shift I work, each patient I care for, presents opportunities to serve on Your behalf. Let my cheerful heart be a dose of Your medicine. Help the joy and peace You give me spill over onto my patients and coworkers. Amen.

COURAGE

I may be compelled to face danger, but never fear it, and while our soldiers can stand and fight, I can stand and feed and nurse them.

CLARA BARTON

Wait on the LORD: be of good courage, and he shall strengthen thine heart: wait, I say, on the LORD.

PSALM 27:14

He giveth power to the faint; and to them that have no might he increaseth strength.   ISAIAH 40:29

The LORD is my strength and my shield; my heart trusted in him, and I am helped: therefore my heart greatly rejoiceth; and with my song will I praise him.   PSALM 28:7

In the fear of the LORD is strong confidence: and his children shall have a place of refuge.

PROVERBS 14:26

For I am persuaded, that neither death, nor life, nor angels, nor principalities, nor powers, nor things present, nor things to come, nor height, nor depth, nor any other creature, shall be able to separate us from the love of God, which is in Christ Jesus our Lord.

ROMANS 8:38–39

Be of good courage,

and he shall strengthen your heart,

all ye that hope in the LORD.

PSALM 31:24

In whom we have boldness and access with confidence by the faith of him.

EPHESIANS 3:12

And he said unto me, My grace is sufficient for thee: for my strength is made perfect in weakness. . . . Therefore I take pleasure in infirmities, in reproaches, in necessities, in persecutions, in distresses for Christ's sake: for when I am weak, then am I strong.

2 CORINTHIANS 12:9–10

I can do all things through Christ which strengtheneth me.   PHILIPPIANS 4:13

"Only be strong and very courageous; be careful to do according to all the law which Moses My servant commanded you; do not turn from it to the right or to the left, so that you may have success wherever you go."   JOSHUA 1:7 NAS

Let integrity and uprightness preserve me; for I wait on thee.   PSALM 25:21

I will go in the strength of the Lord GOD, I will make mention of thy righteousness, even of thine only.   PSALM 71:16

Finally, my brethren, be strong in the Lord, and in the power of his might.   EPHESIANS 6:10

My heart is pounding, and my knees are shaking, Lord. Please keep my hands steady and still my nerves. Give me the ability to face the danger, to do the tasks, to step ahead in faith so I can care for those who need me. Calm my spirit, Lord. Let me set aside my fear and do all I can to help those with whom I'm entrusted. Amen.

DEALING WITH DIFFICULT PEOPLE

*P*eople are often unreasonable, illogical, and self-centered; forgive them anyway. If you are kind, people may accuse you of selfish, ulterior motives; be kind anyway. If you are successful you will win some false friends and true enemies; succeed anyway. If you are honest and frank, people may cheat you; be honest and frank anyway. What you spend years building, someone could destroy overnight; build anyway. If you find serenity and happiness, they may be jealous; be happy anyway. The good you do today, people will often forget tomorrow; do good anyway. Give the world the best you have, and it may never be enough; give the world the best you've got anyway. You see, in the final analysis, it is between you and God; it was never between you and them anyway.

MOTHER TERESA

A soft answer turneth away wrath: but grievous words stir up anger.   PROVERBS 15:1

Do everything without complaining or arguing. . . .
You are living with crooked and mean people all
around you, among whom you shine like stars in
the dark world.   PHILIPPIANS 2:14–15 NCV

We have this treasure from God, but we are like clay
jars that hold the treasure. This shows that the great
power is from God, not from us. We have troubles
all around us, but we are not defeated. We do not
know what to do, but we do not give up the hope
of living. We are persecuted, but God does not leave
us. We are hurt sometimes, but we are not destroyed.
                    2 CORINTHIANS 4:7–9 NCV

We who are strong in faith

should help the weak

with their weaknesses,

and not please only ourselves.

ROMANS 15:1 NCV

But the wisdom that is from above is first pure, then
peaceable, gentle, and easy to be intreated, full of
mercy and good fruits, without partiality, and without hypocrisy.   JAMES 3:17

When a man's ways please the LORD, he maketh even his enemies to be at peace with him.

PROVERBS 16:7

Be ye kind one to another, tenderhearted, forgiving one another, even as God for Christ's sake hath forgiven you.

EPHESIANS 4:32

But the fruit of the Spirit is love, joy, peace, long-suffering, gentleness, goodness, faith, meekness, temperance: against such there is no law. . . . If we live in the Spirit, let us also walk in the Spirit.

GALATIANS 5:22–23, 25

Some people, by always continuing to do good, live for God's glory, for honor, and for life that has no end. . . . He will give trouble and suffering to everyone who does evil.

ROMANS 2:7, 9 NCV

Comfort the feebleminded, support the weak, be patient toward all men. See that none render evil for evil unto any man; but ever follow that which is good, both among yourselves, and to all men.

1 THESSALONIANS 5:14–15

Love. . .is not rude, it is not self-seeking, it is not easily angered, it keeps no record of wrongs. Love does not delight in evil but rejoices with the truth.

1 CORINTHIANS 13:4–6 NIV

Let your conversation be always full of grace, seasoned with salt, so that you may know how to answer everyone. COLOSSIANS 4:6 NIV

Finally, be ye all of one mind, having compassion one of another, love as brethren, be pitiful, be courteous. 1 PETER 3:8

Lord, grant me understanding when dealing with difficult people. Help me to be kind when someone is unpleasant. Let me lean on Your example and cover them in kindness. Help me see past the anger, the demands, the unreasonable behavior and comments. You looked past the sin and saw the soul of the sinner. Help me to open my heart to be a servant instead of digging in my heels. Let me become a peacemaker in Your name. Give me wisdom to say or do the right thing. Let me extend Your mercy and love; let others see Your light shining through me. Amen.

The first time I had a patient die and started to take her down to the morgue, the words of a wise old nun whispered in my mind: "Treat that body gently and with the greatest of respect; it once housed a soul."

CATHY HAKE, RN

Yea, though I walk through the valley of the shadow of death, I will fear no evil: for thou art with me; thy rod and thy staff they comfort me.   PSALM 23:4

O death, where is thy sting? O grave, where is thy victory?   1 CORINTHIANS 15:55

The wicked is driven away in his wickedness: but the righteous hath hope in his death.

PROVERBS 14:32

And God shall wipe away all tears from their eyes; and there shall be no more death, neither sorrow, nor crying, neither shall there be any more pain: for the former things are passed away.

REVELATION 21:4

But I would not have you to be ignorant, brethren, concerning them which are asleep, that ye sorrow not, even as others which have no hope. For if we believe that Jesus died and rose again, even so them also which sleep in Jesus will God bring with him.

1 THESSALONIANS 4:13–14

But God will redeem my soul

from the power of the grave:

for he shall receive me.

PSALM 49:15

Forasmuch then as the children are partakers of flesh and blood, he also himself likewise took part of the same; that through death he might destroy him that had the power of death, that is, the devil; and deliver them who through fear of death were all their lifetime subject to bondage.

HEBREWS 2:14–15

For the Lord himself shall descend from heaven with a shout, with the voice of the archangel, and with the trump of God: and the dead in Christ shall rise first: then we which are alive and remain shall be caught up together with them in the clouds, to meet the Lord in the air: and so shall we ever be with the Lord. Wherefore comfort one another with these words.   1 THESSALONIANS 4:16–18

Much more then, being now justified by his blood, we shall be saved from wrath through him.

ROMANS 5:9

Verily, verily, I say unto you, If a man keep my saying, he shall never see death.   JOHN 8:51

For this God is our God for ever and ever: he will be our guide even unto death.   PSALM 48:14

My flesh and my heart faileth: but God is the strength of my heart, and my portion for ever.

PSALM 73:26

He will swallow up death in victory; and the Lord GOD will wipe away tears from off all faces.

ISAIAH 25:8

I will ransom them from the power of the grave; I will redeem them from death: O death, I will be thy plagues; O grave, I will be thy destruction: repentance shall be hid from mine eyes.   HOSEA 13:14

But though our outward man perish, yet the inward man is renewed day by day.

2 CORINTHIANS 4:16

Precious in the sight of the LORD is the death of his saints.

PSALM 116:15

Mark the perfect man, and behold the upright: for the end of that man is peace.

PSALM 37:37

That whosoever believeth in him should not perish, but have eternal life.

JOHN 3:15

For I am persuaded, that neither death, nor life, nor angels, nor principalities, nor powers, nor things present, nor things to come, nor height, nor depth, nor any other creature, shall be able to separate us from the love of God, which is in Christ Jesus our Lord.

ROMANS 8:38–39

Jesus, You wept upon hearing of Lazarus's death. You understand what it means to lose someone You love. You also know what it was to face death Yourself. Because of You, death has no power. As we walk in the valley of the shadow of death, walk alongside us. Let us be aware of Your comfort, Your promises, and Your compassion. Thank You for the tenderness of Your tears as well as the spilling of Your blood. Both will give us consolation today. Amen.

Volumes are now being written and spoken about the effect of the mind on the body—I wish more was thought of the effect of the body on the mind.

FLORENCE NIGHTINGALE

Why art thou cast down, O my soul? and why art thou disquieted within me? hope thou in God: for I shall yet praise him, who is the health of my countenance, and my God.   PSALM 42:11

The LORD is good, a strong hold in the day of trouble; and he knoweth them that trust in him.

NAHUM 1:7

Though I walk in the midst of trouble, thou wilt revive me.   PSALM 138:7

41

Thou art my hiding place; thou shalt preserve me from trouble; thou shalt encompass me about with songs of deliverance.   PSALM 32:7

He healeth the broken in heart, and bindeth up their wounds.   PSALM 147:3

The LORD also will be a refuge

for the oppressed,

a refuge in times of trouble.

PSALM 9:9

Many are the afflictions of the righteous: but the LORD delivereth him out of them all.
PSALM 34:19

Casting all your care upon him; for he careth for you.   1 PETER 5:7

In the multitude of my thoughts within me thy comforts delight my soul.   PSALM 94:19

A merry heart doeth good like a medicine: but a broken spirit drieth the bones.   PROVERBS 17:22

Likewise the Spirit also helpeth our infirmities: for we know not what we should pray for as we ought: but the Spirit itself maketh intercession for us with groanings which cannot be uttered. And he that searcheth the hearts knoweth what is the mind of the Spirit, because he maketh intercession for the saints according to the will of God.

ROMANS 8:26–27

Where no counsel is, the people fall: but in the multitude of counsellors there is safety.

PROVERBS 11:14

Without counsel purposes are disappointed: but in the multitude of counsellors they are established.

PROVERBS 15:22

A wise man will hear, and will increase learning; and a man of understanding shall attain unto wise counsels.

PROVERBS 1:5

Lord, remind me of Your love for those whose emotional strength wavers. David and Saul. Job. Solomon. They were all Your men, and all struggled with melancholy. Life carries great burdens, and we are not meant to shoulder them alone. In our weakness, You are our strength. In the dark of this emotional night, light the torch and hold my hand. I cannot go on without Your help, God. Amen.

DUTY

In a world where there is so much to be done, I felt strongly impressed that there must be something for me to do.
DOROTHEA DIX

Now therefore fear the LORD, and serve him in sincerity and in truth.   JOSHUA 24:14

And if it seem evil unto you to serve the LORD, choose you this day whom ye will serve. . .but as for me and my house, we will serve the LORD.
JOSHUA 24:15

Now therefore, if ye will obey my voice indeed, and keep my covenant, then ye shall be a peculiar treasure unto me above all people: for all the earth is mine.   EXODUS 19:5

Thou shalt keep therefore his statutes, and his commandments, which I command thee this day, that it may go well with thee, and with thy children after thee, and that thou mayest prolong thy days upon the earth, which the LORD thy God giveth thee, for ever.   DEUTERONOMY 4:40

If ye be willing and obedient,

ye shall eat the good of the land.

ISAIAH 1:19

If they obey and serve him, they shall spend their days in prosperity, and their years in pleasures.
          JOB 36:11

And why call ye me, Lord, Lord, and do not the things which I say?   LUKE 6:46

And shewing mercy unto thousands of them that love me, and keep my commandments.
          EXODUS 20:6

Withhold not good from them to whom it is due, when it is in the power of thine hand to do it.
          PROVERBS 3:27

Observe and hear all these words which I command thee, that it may go well with thee, and with thy children after thee for ever, when thou doest that which is good and right in the sight of the LORD thy God. DEUTERONOMY 12:28

See, I have set before thee this day life and good, and death and evil; in that I command thee this day to love the LORD thy God, to walk in his ways, and to keep his commandments and his statutes and his judgments, that thou mayest live and multiply: and the LORD thy God shall bless thee in the land whither thou goest to possess it.
DEUTERONOMY 30:15–16

Let us hear the conclusion of the whole matter: Fear God, and keep his commandments: for this is the whole duty of man. ECCLESIASTES 12:13

Lord, help me to follow in Your statutes. . .to love You with all my heart. . .to do what is good in Your sight. . .to be fair to all men. . .and to walk humbly before You. Guide me as I extend mercy to those in my care. Let them see not the "duty" of my job, but rather let them see Your love shining through each action and deed. Amen.

"I can do all things through Christ who strengthens me."

NKJV

When I feel tired or impatient, I just pray that Scripture to remind me that I do not have to rely only on my own patience, strength, or endurance. God is there to strengthen me; and since He can do all things, so can I, through Him. It gives me a renewed attitude and optimism in those situations.

ANN ADKINS, RNP

But exhort one another daily, while it is called To day; lest any of you be hardened through the deceitfulness of sin.   HEBREWS 3:13

He giveth power to the faint; and to them that have no might he increaseth strength.   ISAIAH 40:29

Let us hold unswervingly to the hope we profess, for he who promised is faithful. And let us consider how we may spur one another on toward love and good deeds. . . . Let us encourage one another.

HEBREWS 10:23–25 NIV

Holding fast the faithful word as he hath been taught, that he may be able by sound doctrine both to exhort and to convince the gainsayers.

TITUS 1:9

I can do all things through Christ which strengtheneth me.

PHILIPPIANS 4:13

Bear ye one another's burdens, and so fulfil the law of Christ.   GALATIANS 6:2

Therefore, brethren, stand fast, and hold the traditions which ye have been taught, whether by word, or our epistle. Now our Lord Jesus Christ himself, and God, even our Father, which hath loved us, and hath given us everlasting consolation and good hope through grace, comfort your hearts, and stablish you in every good word and work.

2 THESSALONIANS 2:15–17

Wherefore comfort yourselves together, and edify one another, even as also ye do.

1 THESSALONIANS 5:11

Ye are witnesses, and God also, how holily and justly and unblameably we behaved ourselves among you that believe: as ye know how we exhorted and comforted and charged every one of you, as a father doth his children, that ye would walk worthy of God, who hath called you unto his kingdom and glory. For this cause also thank we God without ceasing, because, when ye received the word of God which ye heard of us, ye received it not as the word of men, but as it is in truth, the word of God, which effectually worketh also in you that believe.

1 THESSALONIANS 2:10–13

Look not every man on his own things, but every man also on the things of others.   PHILIPPIANS 2:4

Heavenly Father, allow me to come alongside someone who needs encouragement today. Give me eyes to see when a patient or coworker needs lifting up. Give me a heart like Yours to reach out in support. And if, as the day goes on, I grow weary, bring to my mind all the wondrous things You have done for me so that I will be refreshed, too. Amen.

ER/Trauma

*C*lara Barton's two "rules of action" were "unconcern for what cannot be helped" and "control under pressure."

But the salvation of the righteous is of the LORD: he is their strength in the time of trouble.

PSALM 37:39

The spirit of God hath made me, and the breath of the Almighty hath given me life.   JOB 33:4

Make me to hear joy and gladness; that the bones which thou hast broken may rejoice.   PSALM 51:8

O LORD, by these things men live, and in all these things is the life of my spirit: so wilt thou recover me, and make me to live.   ISAIAH 38:16

Many are the afflictions of the righteous: but the LORD delivereth him out of them all. He keepeth all his bones: not one of them is broken.

PSALM 34:19–20

But a certain Samaritan, as he journeyed, came where he was: and when he saw him, he had compassion on him.   LUKE 10:33

Speak up for those who cannot speak for themselves; ensure justice for those who are perishing. Yes, speak up for the poor and helpless, and see that they get justice.   PROVERBS 31:8–9 NLT

I have shewed you all things, how that so labouring ye ought to support the weak, and to remember the words of the Lord Jesus, how he said, It is more blessed to give than to receive.   ACTS 20:35

And beside this, giving all diligence, add to your faith virtue; and to virtue knowledge; and to knowledge temperance; and to temperance patience; and to patience godliness; and to godliness brotherly kindness; and to brotherly kindness charity. For if these things be in you, and abound, they make you that ye shall neither be barren nor unfruitful in the knowledge of our Lord Jesus Christ. 2 PETER 1:5–8

But though he cause grief, yet will he have compassion according to the multitude of his mercies.

LAMENTATIONS 3:32

Waters flowed over mine head; then I said, I am cut off. I called upon thy name, O LORD, out of the low dungeon. Thou hast heard my voice: hide not thine ear at my breathing, at my cry. Thou drewest near in the day that I called upon thee: thou saidst, Fear not. O LORD, thou hast pleaded the causes of my soul; thou hast redeemed my life.

LAMENTATIONS 3:54–58

These things will happen when
the Lord bandages
his broken people
and heals the hurts he gave them.

ISAIAH 30: 26 NCV

Heal me, O LORD, and I shall be healed; save me, and I shall be saved: for thou art my praise.

JEREMIAH 17:14

There shall no evil befall thee, neither shall any plague come nigh thy dwelling. PSALM 91:10

God is our refuge and strength, a very present help in trouble. PSALM 46:1

He took his stand between the dead and the living, so that the plague was checked.

NUMBERS 16:48 NAS

Come, and let us return unto the LORD: for he hath torn, and he will heal us; he hath smitten, and he will bind us up. HOSEA 6:1

And said, I cried by reason of mine affliction unto the LORD, and he heard me; out of the belly of hell cried I, and thou heardest my voice. JONAH 2:2

"Do not be afraid nor dismayed because of this great multitude, for the battle is not yours, but God's."

2 CHRONICLES 20:15 NKJV

I'm the first stop, Lord. Something unexpected happened, something bad. They come to me bleeding, battered, or breathless. They're hurting and frightened. Everything needs to be done now. Each decision matters. Make me the calm in the middle of the storm and help me to help them. Many of them have called out to You—some are Your children, some are not. Let me reflect You to them. In the midst of all of the technical and medical interventions, remind me to still remember that Christ healed with His words and touch. Use me, Lord—my mind, my abilities, my words, and my touch. Amen.

ETERNAL LIFE

S *ome of our patients pass from our hands into God's. It is an honor to escort them into His presence. Only God knows their hearts, but we can speak the promises of repentance as a last opportunity. Because of Christ's sacrifice, we have the assurance that our Christian patients have the gift of eternal life.*

TRACEY LARSON, RN

Verily, verily, I say unto you, He that believeth on me hath everlasting life. JOHN 6:47

Jesus said unto her, I am the resurrection, and the life: he that believeth in me, though he were dead, yet shall he live: and whosoever liveth and believeth in me shall never die. Believest thou this?

JOHN 11:25–26

And this is the promise that he hath promised us, even eternal life.   1 JOHN 2:25

Behold, I shew you a mystery; We shall not all sleep, but we shall all be changed, in a moment, in the twinkling of an eye, at the last trump: for the trumpet shall sound, and the dead shall be raised incorruptible, and we shall be changed. For this corruptible must put on incorruption, and this mortal must put on immortality. So when this corruptible shall have put on incorruption, and this mortal shall have put on immortality, then shall be brought to pass the saying that is written, Death is swallowed up in victory.   1 CORINTHIANS 15:51–54

For since by man came death, by man came also the resurrection of the dead.   1 CORINTHIANS 15:21

For the Lord himself shall descend from heaven with a shout, with the voice of the archangel, and with the trump of God: and the dead in Christ shall rise first.   1 THESSALONIANS 4:16

These things have I written unto you that believe on the name of the Son of God; that ye may know that ye have eternal life, and that ye may believe on the name of the Son of God.   1 JOHN 5:13

For he that soweth to his flesh shall of the flesh reap corruption; but he that soweth to the Spirit shall of the Spirit reap life everlasting.   GALATIANS 6:8

Marvel not at this: for the hour is coming, in the which all that are in the graves shall hear his voice, and shall come forth; they that have done good, unto the resurrection of life; and they that have done evil, unto the resurrection of damnation.

JOHN 5:28–29

For the wages of sin is death;

but the gift of God is

eternal life through

Jesus Christ our Lord.

ROMANS 6:23

And many of them that sleep in the dust of the earth shall awake, some to everlasting life, and some to shame and everlasting contempt.   DANIEL 12:2

So also is the resurrection of the dead. It is sown in corruption; it is raised in incorruption: It is sown in dishonour; it is raised in glory: it is sown in weakness; it is raised in power: It is sown a natural body; it is raised a spiritual body. There is a natural body, and there is a spiritual body.

1 CORINTHIANS 15:42–44

Therefore are they before the throne of God, and serve him day and night in his temple: and he that sitteth on the throne shall dwell among them. They shall hunger no more, neither thirst any more; neither shall the sun light on them, nor any heat. For the Lamb which is in the midst of the throne shall feed them, and shall lead them unto living fountains of waters: and God shall wipe away all tears from their eyes.   REVELATION 7:15–17

But if the Spirit of him that raised up Jesus from the dead dwell in you, he that raised up Christ from the dead shall also quicken your mortal bodies by his Spirit that dwelleth in you.   ROMANS 8:11

And God shall wipe away all tears from their eyes; and there shall be no more death, neither sorrow, nor crying, neither shall there be any more pain: for the former things are passed away.   REVELATION 21:4

But is now made manifest by the appearing of our Saviour Jesus Christ, who hath abolished death, and hath brought life and immortality to light through the gospel.   2 TIMOTHY 1:10

In my Father's house are many mansions: if it were not so, I would have told you. I go to prepare a place for you. And if I go and prepare a place for you, I will come again, and receive you unto myself; that where I am, there ye may be also.   JOHN 14:2–3

For we know that if our earthly house of this tabernacle were dissolved, we have a building of God, an house not made with hands, eternal in the heavens.
2 CORINTHIANS 5:1

Thy dead men shall live, together with my dead body shall they arise. Awake and sing, ye that dwell in dust: for thy dew is as the dew of herbs, and the earth shall cast out the dead. ISAIAH 26:19

And this is the record, that God hath given to us eternal life, and this life is in his Son. 1 JOHN 5:11

Nevertheless we, according to his promise, look for new heavens and a new earth, wherein dwelleth righteousness. 2 PETER 3:13

And I give unto them eternal life; and they shall never perish, neither shall any man pluck them out of my hand. JOHN 10:28

And when the chief Shepherd shall appear, ye shall receive a crown of glory that fadeth not away.
1 PETER 5:4

And I saw a new heaven and a new earth: for the first heaven and the first earth were passed away; and there was no more sea. And I John saw the holy city, new Jerusalem, coming down from God out of heaven, prepared as a bride adorned for her husband. REVELATION 21:1–2

Henceforth there is laid up for me a crown of righteousness, which the Lord, the righteous judge, shall give me at that day: and not to me only, but unto all them also that love his appearing.   2 TIMOTHY 4:8

Verily, verily, I say unto you, He that heareth my word, and believeth on him that sent me, hath everlasting life, and shall not come into condemnation; but is passed from death unto life.   JOHN 5:24

He that loveth his life

shall lose it;

and he that hateth his life

in this world shall keep it

unto life eternal.

JOHN 12:25

Search the scriptures; for in them ye think ye have eternal life: and they are they which testify of me.
JOHN 5:39

And there shall be no night there; and they need no candle, neither light of the sun; for the Lord God giveth them light: and they shall reign for ever and ever.   REVELATION 22:5

Blessed be the God and Father of our Lord Jesus Christ, which according to his abundant mercy hath begotten us again unto a lively hope by the resurrection of Jesus Christ from the dead, to an inheritance incorruptible, and undefiled, and that fadeth not away, reserved in heaven for you, who are kept by the power of God through faith unto salvation ready to be revealed in the last time.

1 PETER 1:3–5

Father, from You I have received the gift of life—for all eternity. Not because of anything I have done, but simply because You love me. Lord, give me a heart like Yours—one that hungers to share Your message of grace and mercy to those who are lost. Let me be light in a world filled with darkness and suffering. Amen.

Faith is stepping out and relying on God's promises. He never fails us. Salvation is the first step, but faith is a continuing walk. Moving ahead, accomplishing things, and growing are all dependent on continuing to believe in His grace, mercy, and desire for our ultimate welfare.

CATHY HAKE, RN

For by grace are ye saved through faith; and that not of yourselves: it is the gift of God.

EPHESIANS 2:8

Now faith is the substance of things hoped for, the evidence of things not seen.   HEBREWS 11:1

Watch ye, stand fast in the faith, quit you like men, be strong.   1 CORINTHIANS 16:13

As ye have therefore received Christ Jesus the Lord, so walk ye in him: rooted and built up in him, and stablished in the faith, as ye have been taught, abounding therein with thanksgiving.

COLOSSIANS 2:6–7

For ye are all the children of God by faith in Christ Jesus. GALATIANS 3:26

So then faith cometh by hearing, and hearing by the word of God. ROMANS 10:17

The fruit of the Spirit is love, joy, peace, longsuffering, gentleness, goodness, faith, meekness, temperance: against such there is no law.

GALATIANS 5:22–23

But continue thou in the things which thou hast learned and hast been assured of, knowing of whom thou hast learned them; and that from a child thou hast known the holy scriptures, which are able to make thee wise unto salvation through faith which is in Christ Jesus. 2 TIMOTHY 3:14–15

For we walk by faith, not by sight.

2 CORINTHIANS 5:7

But as many as received him, to them gave he power to become the sons of God, even to them that believe on his name. JOHN 1:12

And Jesus answering saith unto them, Have faith in God. For verily I say unto you, That whosoever shall say unto this mountain, Be thou removed, and be thou cast into the sea; and shall not doubt in his heart, but shall believe that those things which he saith shall come to pass; he shall have whatsoever he saith. Mark 11:22–23

That Christ may dwell in your hearts by faith; that ye, being rooted and grounded in love, may be able to comprehend with all saints what is the breadth, and length, and depth, and height; and to know the love of Christ, which passeth knowledge, that ye might be filled with all the fulness of God.

Ephesians 3:17–19

That your faith should not stand in the wisdom of men, but in the power of God.

1 Corinthians 2:5

That if thou shalt confess with thy mouth the Lord Jesus, and shalt believe in thine heart that God hath raised him from the dead, thou shalt be saved.

Romans 10:9

I am crucified with Christ: nevertheless I live; yet not I, but Christ liveth in me: and the life which I now live in the flesh I live by the faith of the Son of God, who loved me, and gave himself for me.

GALATIANS 2:20

Wherefore seeing we also are compassed about with so great a cloud of witnesses, let us lay aside every weight, and the sin which doth so easily beset us, and let us run with patience the race that is set before us, looking unto Jesus the author and finisher of our faith; who for the joy that was set before him endured the cross, despising the shame, and is set down at the right hand of the throne of God.

HEBREWS 12:1–2

Whom having not seen, ye love; in whom, though now ye see him not, yet believing, ye rejoice with joy unspeakable and full of glory. 1 PETER 1:8

He that believeth and is baptized shall be saved.

MARK 16:16

Jesus said unto him, If thou canst believe, all things are possible to him that believeth. MARK 9:23

But without faith it is impossible to please him: for he that cometh to God must believe that he is, and that he is a rewarder of them that diligently seek him. HEBREWS 11:6

Let us draw near with a true heart in full assurance of faith, having our hearts sprinkled from an evil conscience, and our bodies washed with pure water.
HEBREWS 10:22

As ye have therefore received Christ Jesus the Lord, so walk ye in him.
COLOSSIANS 2:6–7

Jesus saith unto her, Said I not unto thee, that, if thou wouldest believe, thou shouldest see the glory of God?
JOHN 11:40

The life which I now live in the flesh I live by the faith of the Son of God, who loved me, and gave himself for me.
GALATIANS 2:20

Behold, I stand at the door, and knock: if any man hear my voice, and open the door, I will come in to him, and will sup with him, and he with me.
REVELATION 3:20

Father, give me eyes to see what is unseen. Renew in me Your steadfast Spirit, and create afresh the desire to know You more. Grant to me again the joy of Your salvation, precious Lord. Fill me with Your love so that I might be salt and light in a dark world. Amen.

FEAR

How very little can be done under the spirit of fear.

FLORENCE NIGHTINGALE

For God hath not given us the spirit of fear; but of power, and of love, and of a sound mind.

2 TIMOTHY 1:7

So that we may boldly say, The Lord is my helper, and I will not fear what man shall do unto me.

HEBREWS 13:6

In righteousness shalt thou be established: thou shalt be far from oppression; for thou shalt not fear: and from terror; for it shall not come near thee.

ISAIAH 54:14

The angel of the LORD encampeth round about them that fear him, and delivereth them.

PSALM 34:7

When thou liest down, thou shalt not be afraid: yea, thou shalt lie down, and thy sleep shall be sweet.

PROVERBS 3:24

He will fulfil the desire of them that fear him: he also will hear their cry, and will save them.

PSALM 145:19

In the fear of the LORD is strong confidence: and his children shall have a place of refuge.

PROVERBS 14:26

The wicked flee when no man pursueth: but the righteous are bold as a lion.   PROVERBS 28:1

Having therefore, brethren, boldness to enter into the holiest by the blood of Jesus.   HEBREWS 10:19

And he said unto them, Why are ye so fearful? how is it that ye have no faith?   MARK 4:40

Fear not, little flock; for it is your Father's good pleasure to give you the kingdom.   LUKE 12:32

For I the LORD thy God will hold thy right hand, saying unto thee, Fear not; I will help thee.

ISAIAH 41:13

But whoso hearkeneth unto me shall dwell safely, and shall be quiet from fear of evil.   PROVERBS 1:33

And fear not them which kill the body, but are not able to kill the soul.   MATTHEW 10:28

Be not afraid of sudden fear, neither of the desolation of the wicked, when it cometh.
For the LORD shall be thy confidence, and shall keep thy foot from being taken.
PROVERBS 3:25–26

I will both lay me down

in peace, and sleep:

for thou, LORD,

only makest me dwell in safety.

PSALM 4:8

For ye have not received the spirit of bondage again to fear; but ye have received the Spirit of adoption, whereby we cry, Abba, Father.   ROMANS 8:15

God is our refuge and strength, a very present help in trouble.   PSALM 46:1

The fear of man bringeth a snare: but whoso putteth his trust in the LORD shall be safe.

PROVERBS 29:25

When thou passest through the waters, I will be with thee; and through the rivers, they shall not overflow thee: when thou walkest through the fire, thou shalt not be burned; neither shall the flame kindle upon thee. ISAIAH 43:2

Peace I leave with you, my peace I give unto you: not as the world giveth, give I unto you. Let not your heart be troubled, neither let it be afraid.

JOHN 14:27

Yea, though I walk through the valley of the shadow of death, I will fear no evil: for thou art with me; thy rod and thy staff they comfort me.

PSALM 23:4

Therefore take no thought, saying, What shall we eat? or, What shall we drink? or, Wherewithal shall we be clothed? (For after all these things do the Gentiles seek:) for your heavenly Father knoweth that ye have need of all these things.

MATTHEW 6:31–32

When I am afraid, I will trust in you. In God, whose word I praise, in God I trust; I will not be afraid. PSALM 56: 3–4 NIV

Fear not; for thou shalt not be ashamed: neither be thou confounded.   ISAIAH 54:4

Lord, You alone can calm my fears. I know nothing happens that hasn't first been through Your throne room, Father. Grant me the peace that only comes from Your hand. Make Your presence evident to me and let me draw upon Your assurance, wisdom, and strength. Keep my eyes focused on what is eternal and not on the circumstances that surround me. Help me to trust You more. Give me strength and grant me peace, knowing You are with me and will see me through. Thank You for Your great mercy and love. Amen.

If the wounds of millions are to be healed, what other way is there except through forgiveness?

CATHERINE MARSHALL

But I say unto you, Love your enemies, bless them that curse you, do good to them that hate you, and pray for them which despitefully use you, and persecute you; that ye may be the children of your Father which is in heaven: for he maketh his sun to rise on the evil and on the good, and sendeth rain on the just and on the unjust.   MATTHEW 5:44–45

And if any man sin, we have an advocate with the Father, Jesus Christ the righteous: and he is the propitiation for our sins: and not for ours only, but also for the sins of the whole world.   1 JOHN 2:1–2

And when ye stand praying, forgive, if ye have ought against any: that your Father also which is in heaven may forgive you your trespasses. But if ye do not forgive, neither will your Father which is in heaven forgive your trespasses.   MARK 11:25–26

For if ye forgive men

their trespasses,

your heavenly Father will also

forgive you.

MATTHEW 6:14

And be ye kind one to another, tenderhearted, forgiving one another, even as God for Christ's sake hath forgiven you.   EPHESIANS 4:32

Forbearing one another, and forgiving one another, if any man have a quarrel against any: even as Christ forgave you, so also do ye.   COLOSSIANS 3:13

And forgive us our sins; for we also forgive every one that is indebted to us. And lead us not into temptation; but deliver us from evil.   LUKE 11:4

Therefore if thine enemy hunger, feed him; if he thirst, give him drink.   ROMANS 12:20

The discretion of a man deferreth his anger; and it is his glory to pass over a transgression.

PROVERBS 19:11

But love ye your enemies, and do good, and lend, hoping for nothing again; and your reward shall be great, and ye shall be the children of the Highest: for he is kind unto the unthankful and to the evil. Be ye therefore merciful, as your Father also is merciful. Judge not, and ye shall not be judged: condemn not, and ye shall not be condemned: forgive, and ye shall be forgiven.   LUKE 6:35–38

Father, I've been hurt. In this moment, the last thing I want to do is to forgive. But even as I hesitate, I know that at the core of forgiveness is the very heart of God. Grant me the strength to forgive another as you have so freely forgiven me. Give me the love to do it in Your name and to be set free from lingering hurt by Your grace. Amen.

GERIATRICS

I have come to realize more and more that the greatest dis-ease and the greatest suffering is to be unwanted, unloved, uncared for, to be shunned by everybody, to be just nobody.

MOTHER TERESA

My flesh and my heart faileth: but God is the strength of my heart, and my portion for ever.

PSALM 73:26

Ye shall walk in all the ways which the LORD your God hath commanded you, that ye may live, and that it may be well with you, and that ye may prolong your days in the land which ye shall possess.

DEUTERONOMY 5:33

Cast me not off in the time of old age; forsake me not when my strength faileth.

PSALM 71:9

I have been young, and now am old; yet have I not seen the righteous forsaken, nor his seed begging bread.   PSALM 37:25

The glory of young men is their strength: and the beauty of old men is the grey head.

PROVERBS 20:29

Children's children are the crown of old men; and the glory of children are their fathers.

PROVERBS 17:6

And thine age shall be clearer than the noonday: thou shalt shine forth, thou shalt be as the morning.

JOB 11:17

And even to your old age I am he. . . . I have made, and I will bear; even I will carry, and will deliver you.   ISAIAH 46:4

Now we exhort you, brethren, warn them that are unruly, comfort the feebleminded, support the weak, be patient toward all men.   1 THESSALONIANS 5:14

O God, thou hast taught me from my youth: and hitherto have I declared thy wondrous works. Now also when I am old and greyheaded, O God, forsake me not; until I have shewed thy strength unto this generation, and thy power to every one that is to come.   PSALM 71:17–18

LORD, make me to know mine end, and the measure of my days, what it is: that I may know how frail I am. Behold, thou hast made my days as an handbreadth; and mine age is as nothing before thee.

PSALM 39:4–5

"With long life I will satisfy him,

And show him My salvation."

PSALM 91:16 NKJV

That thou mightest fear the LORD thy God, to keep all his statutes and his commandments, which I command thee, thou, and thy son, and thy son's son, all the days of thy life; and that thy days may be prolonged. DEUTERONOMY 6:2

Ageless God, use me as a willing vessel so I can pour out Your love, caring, and help to those who are in need. My world moves so fast, yet those whom I'm to care for are slowed by years and infirmities. Give me patience. Make my hands and heart tender, and help me to show respect as I care for these old folks. Amen.

God is always there for me. He's faithful in all things—both large and small. I want to be willing to be a servant for Him, to attend to details as diligently and lovingly as He does, as I care for others.

PEGGY O'BRIEN, RN

Let us hold fast the profession of our faith without wavering; (for he is faithful that promised).

HEBREWS 10:23

"For the LORD your God is a compassionate God; He will not fail you nor destroy you nor forget the covenant with your fathers which He swore to them." DEUTERONOMY 4:31 NAS

My covenant will I not break, nor alter the thing that is gone out of my lips. PSALM 89:34

He hath remembered his covenant for ever, the word which he commanded to a thousand generations.

PSALM 105:8

Let us hold fast the confession of our hope without wavering, for He who promised is faithful.

HEBREWS 10:23 NAS

*Thy word is true
from the beginning:
and every one of thy
righteous judgments
endureth for ever.*

PSALM 119:160

If we are not faithful, he will still be faithful, because he cannot be false to himself.

2 TIMOTHY 2:13 NCV

The Lord is not slack concerning his promise, as some men count slackness; but is longsuffering to us-ward, not willing that any should perish, but that all should come to repentance.   2 PETER 3:9

Know therefore that the LORD thy God, he is God, the faithful God, which keepeth covenant and mercy with them that love him and keep his commandments to a thousand generations.

DEUTERONOMY 7:9

O LORD, thou art my God; I will exalt thee, I will praise thy name; for thou hast done wonderful things; thy counsels of old are faithfulness and truth.

ISAIAH 25:1

And they that know thy name will put their trust in thee: for thou, LORD, hast not forsaken them that seek thee.

PSALM 9:10

For ever, O LORD, thy word is settled in heaven. Thy faithfulness is unto all generations.

PSALM 119:89–90

For all the promises of God in him are yea, and in him Amen, unto the glory of God by us.

2 CORINTHIANS 1:20

Lord, I rejoice in knowing Your promises are true. Your Word is always before me, keeping my path straight, encouraging me to go forward in Your strength. Thank You for Your faithfulness and never-ending love. I praise You for Your holiness, Your righteousness, and Your loving-kindness. Amen.

Nursing, most of all, gives me an opportunity to explore and share my God-given potential—whether at the bedside of a critically ill patient, teaching, or mentoring a novice nurse. I know He created me with a purpose to do the best I can for the service and love of others. The work I do every day reminds me how blessed I am to share His love.

CECILE P. JALANDONI, RN CCRN,
KAISER PERMANENTE, ORANGE COUNTY

That Christ may dwell in your hearts by faith; that ye, being rooted and grounded in love, may be able to comprehend with all saints what is the breadth, and length, and depth, and height; and to know the love of Christ, which passeth knowledge, that ye might be filled with all the fulness of God.

EPHESIANS 3:17–19

But as it is written, Eye hath not seen, nor ear heard, neither have entered into the heart of man, the things which God hath prepared for them that love him.   1 CORINTHIANS 2:9

Behold, what manner of love the Father hath bestowed upon us, that we should be called the sons of God.   1 JOHN 3:1

In this was manifested the love of God toward us, because that God sent his only begotten Son into the world, that we might live through him.
                                              1 JOHN 4:9

And we have known and believed the love that God hath to us. God is love; and he that dwelleth in love dwelleth in God, and God in him.
                                              1 JOHN 4:16

For the Father himself loveth you, because ye have loved me, and have believed that I came out from God.   JOHN 16:27

And I have declared unto them thy name, and will declare it: that the love wherewith thou hast loved me may be in them, and I in them.   JOHN 17:26

The LORD thy God in the midst of thee is mighty; he will save, he will rejoice over thee with joy; he will rest in his love, he will joy over thee with singing.
                                              ZEPHANIAH 3:17

The LORD hath appeared of old unto me, saying, Yea, I have loved thee with an everlasting love: therefore with lovingkindness have I drawn thee.

JEREMIAH 31:3

But God, who is rich in mercy, because of His great love with which He loved us, even when we were dead in trespasses, made us alive together with Christ (by grace you have been saved), and raised us up together, and made us sit together in the heavenly places in Christ Jesus, that in the ages to come He might show the exceeding riches of His grace in His kindness toward us in Christ Jesus.

EPHESIANS 2:4–7 NKJV

We love him,

because he first loved us.

1 JOHN 4:19

For the Father himself loveth you, because ye have loved me, and have believed that I came out from God.

JOHN 16:27

And hope maketh not ashamed; because the love of God is shed abroad in our hearts by the Holy Ghost which is given unto us.

ROMANS 5:5

As the Father hath loved me, so have I loved you: continue ye in my love.   JOHN 15:9

Now our Lord Jesus Christ himself, and God, even our Father, which hath loved us, and hath given us everlasting consolation and good hope through grace, comfort your hearts, and stablish you in every good word and work.   2 THESSALONIANS 2:16–17

For I am persuaded, that neither death, nor life, nor angels, nor principalities, nor powers, nor things present, nor things to come, nor height, nor depth, nor any other creature, shall be able to separate us from the love of God, which is in Christ Jesus our Lord.   ROMANS 8:38–39

Measureless and free is Your love, kind Father. You, who hold life and time in Your hands, care for me. How thankful I am that my soul belongs to You! How glad I am that You provided the means to redeem me, so I could walk in the sunshine of Your everlasting love. Amen.

GOSSIP

When Clara Barton, the founder of the American Red Cross, was reminded of something someone did to her, she responded, "I don't remember that." When told she must remember it, she replied, "I distinctly remember forgetting that."

Even so the tongue is a little member, and boasteth great things. Behold, how great a matter a little fire kindleth!   JAMES 3:5

The heart of the righteous studieth to answer: but the mouth of the wicked poureth out evil things.
PROVERBS 15:28

A fool uttereth all his mind: but a wise man keepeth it in till afterwards.   PROVERBS 29:11

But now ye also put off all these; anger, wrath, malice, blasphemy, filthy communication out of your mouth. COLOSSIANS 3:8

There is that speaketh like the piercings of a sword: but the tongue of the wise is health.

PROVERBS 12:18

Thou shalt not go up and down as a talebearer among thy people: neither shalt thou stand against the blood of thy neighbour: I am the LORD.

LEVITICUS 19:16

The words of a talebearer are as wounds, and they go down into the innermost parts of the belly.

PROVERBS 18:8

He that goeth about as a talebearer revealeth secrets: therefore meddle not with him that flattereth with his lips. PROVERBS 20:19

A talebearer revealeth secrets: but he that is of a faithful spirit concealeth the matter.

PROVERBS 11:13

A perverse man stirs up dissension, and a gossip separates close friends. PROVERBS 16:28 NIV

The tongue deviseth mischiefs; like a sharp razor, working deceitfully. PSALM 52:2

Where no wood is, there the fire goeth out: so where there is no talebearer, the strife ceaseth. As coals are to burning coals, and wood to fire; so is a contentious man to kindle strife. The words of a talebearer are as wounds, and they go down into the innermost parts of the belly.   PROVERBS 26:20–22

As the north wind brings rain, telling gossip brings angry looks.   PROVERBS 25:23 NCV

Keep thy tongue from evil, and thy lips from speaking guile.   PSALM 34:13

The heart of him that hath understanding seeketh knowledge: but the mouth of fools feedeth on foolishness.   PROVERBS 15:14

Lord of heaven and earth, make me mindful of my words. Help me to keep private matters private. Halt my tongue and keep me from speaking to others when an issue needs to be kept between myself and another. Keep me silent when an issue is none of my affair. Instead of fanning the flames or warming my hands by the fire, help me to speak words of kindness, forgiveness, and peace. Amen.

So much is written about helping the patients and families deal with loss. Nurses deal with loss, too. It can be especially hard when we've cared for someone long-term and come to know them well. Nursing opens us up to the joy of helping others heal—but the sad truth is, it also makes us vulnerable to caring deeply and having to let go.

CATHY M. HAKE, RN, BS,
ONCOLOGY NURSE

For ye have not received the spirit of bondage again to fear; but ye have received the Spirit of adoption, whereby we cry, Abba, Father. ROMANS 8:15

The LORD is nigh unto them that are of a broken heart; and saveth such as be of a contrite spirit.
PSALM 34:18

God is our refuge and strength, an ever-present help
in trouble. PSALM 46:1 NIV

The Lord GOD will wipe away tears from off all
faces. ISAIAH 25:8

The Lord defends those who suffer; he defends
them in times of trouble. PSALM 9:9 NCV

Trust in him at all times, O people; pour out your
hearts to him, for God is our refuge.
PSALM 62:8 NIV

Weeping may endure for a night, but joy cometh
in the morning. PSALM 30:5

Cast your cares on the LORD and he will sustain
you. PSALM 55:22 NIV

Behold, I shew you a mystery; We shall not all sleep,
but we shall all be changed, in a moment, in the
twinkling of an eye, at the last trump: for the trumpet shall sound, and the dead shall be raised incorruptible, and we shall be changed. . . . Death is
swallowed up in victory. O death, where is thy sting?
O grave, where is thy victory?
1 CORINTHIANS 15:51–52, 54–55

The LORD upholds all those who fall and lifts up
all who are bowed down. PSALM 145:14 NIV

A father to the fatherless, a defender of widows, is God in his holy dwelling. PSALM 68:5 NIV

Blessed be God, even the Father of our Lord Jesus Christ, the Father of mercies, and the God of all comfort; who comforteth us in all our tribulation, that we may be able to comfort them which are in any trouble, by the comfort wherewith we ourselves are comforted of God. 2 CORINTHIANS 1:3–4

Blessed are they that mourn:

for they shall be comforted.

MATTHEW 5:4

He who dwells in the shelter of the Most High will rest in the shadow of the Almighty. I will say of the LORD, "He is my refuge and my fortress, my God, in whom I trust." PSALM 91:1–2 NIV

I am still confident of this: I will see the goodness of the LORD in the land of the living. Wait for the LORD; be strong and take heart and wait for the LORD. PSALM 27:13–14 NIV

Father, there is both good and bad, joy and sorrow in our walk here on earth. Help me to understand and trust You through this painful time, to reach out to You for solace. Thank You for Your love, Your mercy, and Your faithfulness even during these difficult days. Guide me on this journey; let my hope in You be complete. When You call someone home, as I console others in Your name, please wrap me in a blanket of Your solace. And when the sun shines again, let me extend comfort to those who are also experiencing grief and loss. Lord, help me to care even if it opens me to hurt. Give me the strength to reach out in Your name, to gently tend to my patients and their loved ones. Amen.

*A*t the age of twenty-four, Florence Nightingale wrote in her journal, "God spoke to me and called me to His service." If we are to be His servants, we must first seek His direction and be devoted to His will. Under that guidance, the opportunity to devote our hours to nursing becomes an immeasurable blessing.

Thy word is a lamp unto my feet, and a light unto my path.   PSALM 119:105

The steps of a good man are ordered by the LORD: and he delighteth in his way.   PSALM 37:23

Whoever gives heed to instruction prospers, and blessed is he who trusts in the LORD.

PROVERBS 16:20 NIV

A man's heart deviseth his way: but the LORD directeth his steps.   PROVERBS 16:9

Trust in the LORD with all thine heart; and lean not unto thine own understanding. In all thy ways acknowledge him, and he shall direct thy paths.
                                   PROVERBS 3:5–6

And I will bring the blind by a way that they knew not; I will lead them in paths that they have not known: I will make darkness light before them, and crooked things straight. These things will I do unto them, and not forsake them.   ISAIAH 42:16

For this God is our God

for ever and ever:

he will be our guide

even unto death.

PSALM 48:14

He will call upon me, and I will answer him; I will be with him in trouble, I will deliver him and honor him.   PSALM 91:15 NIV

For his God doth instruct him to discretion, and doth teach him.   ISAIAH 28:26

Listen to advice and accept instruction, and in the end you will be wise.   PROVERBS 19:20 NIV

I will instruct you and teach you in the way you should go; I will counsel you and watch over you.
                                        PSALM 32:8 NIV

The Bible talks of symbols of Your guidance—a pillar of smoke, fire, maidens with lamps. . . Holy Healer, guide me as I work today. Guide my steps to the bedsides of those who need my touch. Sharpen my senses so my assessments are swift. Bring to mind the knowledge I've gained and grant Your wisdom so my decisions are sound. Guide me, my great Jehovah. I am lost without You. Amen.

Never feel guilty for showing genuine compassion, regardless of the circumstance.

ELVERA SMITH, RN

He who conceals his sins does not prosper, but whoever confesses and renounces them finds mercy.

PROVERBS 28:13 NIV

I, even I, am he that blotteth out thy transgressions for mine own sake, and will not remember thy sins.

ISAIAH 43:25

Then I acknowledged my sin to you and did not cover up my iniquity. I said, "I will confess my transgressions to the LORD"—and you forgave the guilt of my sin.

PSALM 32:5 NIV

I will put my laws into their hearts, and in their minds I will write them; and their sins and iniquities will I remember no more.   HEBREWS 10:16–17

For thou, Lord, art good, and ready to forgive; and plenteous in mercy unto all them that call upon thee.   PSALM 86:5

As far as the east is from the west,

so far hath he removed

our transgressions from us.

PSALM 103:12

Help us, O God of our salvation, for the glory of thy name: and deliver us, and purge away our sins, for thy name's sake.   PSALM 79:9

Remember not the sins of my youth, nor my transgressions: according to thy mercy remember thou me for thy goodness' sake, O LORD.   PSALM 25:7

For I will be merciful to their unrighteousness, and their sins and their iniquities will I remember no more.   HEBREWS 8:12

For if our heart condemn us, God is greater than our heart, and knoweth all things.   1 JOHN 3:20

Lord, I know that when I come to You with my failure, You are faithful to forgive. Help me to let go of the burden of my guilt, to embrace Your abundant mercy. Remove the anxiety and let the refreshing purity of Your Holy Spirit cleanse my thoughts, that I might again serve You without hesitation. Amen.

I attribute my success to this—I never gave or took any excuse.

FLORENCE NIGHTINGALE

Be of the same mind one toward another. . . . Recompense to no man evil for evil. Provide things honest in the sight of all men.   ROMANS 12:16–17

Pray for us: for we trust we have a good conscience, in all things willing to live honestly.

HEBREWS 13:18

Who shall ascend into the hill of the LORD? or who shall stand in his holy place? He that hath clean hands, and a pure heart; who hath not lifted up his soul unto vanity, nor sworn deceitfully.

PSALM 24:3–4

Lie not one to another, seeing that ye have put off the old man with his deeds; and have put on the new man, which is renewed in knowledge after the image of him that created him.   COLOSSIANS 3:9–10

Blessed is the man unto whom the LORD imputeth not iniquity, and in whose spirit there is no guile.
PSALM 32:2

Providing for honest things,

not only in the sight of the Lord,

but also in the sight of men.

2 CORINTHIANS 8:21

And in their mouth was found no guile: for they are without fault before the throne of God.
REVELATION 14:5

My righteousness I hold fast, and will not let it go: my heart shall not reproach me so long as I live.
JOB 27:6

Ye shall do no unrighteousness in judgment, in meteyard, in weight, or in measure.
LEVITICUS 19:35

Ye shall not steal, neither deal falsely, neither lie one to another. LEVITICUS 19:11

That no man go beyond and defraud his brother in any matter: because that the Lord is the avenger of all such, as we also have forewarned you and testified. For God hath not called us unto uncleanness, but unto holiness. 1 THESSALONIANS 4:6–7

Better is a little with righteousness than great revenues without right. PROVERBS 16:8

Finally, brethren, whatsoever things are true, whatsoever things are honest, whatsoever things are just, whatsoever things are pure, whatsoever things are lovely, whatsoever things are of good report; if there be any virtue, and if there be any praise, think on these things. PHILIPPIANS 4:8

It's easy to rationalize things, to make excuses, to shrug off responsibilities. I don't want to take the easy path, Father. I want to be honorable, to be honest. Empower me to complete each task to the best of my ability, to report clearly and honestly what transpires, and to speak truth even when the words are difficult. I'm Your child and represent Your integrity and truth. Stand alongside me to keep me strong and accountable, I pray. Amen.

HOPE

The nursing profession is built on hope—the hope that things can and will get better. The Christian nurse has the ultimate hope, because she works with her hand in God's.
CATHY HAKE, RN

Positive thinking affects not only our happiness but our health. We get what we expect in life—what we think about. Our thoughts control our actions, which affect our outcomes. A positive attitude and strong faith make all of the difference—often in the physical outcome, but always in the emotional and spiritual.

LEANN THIEMAN, LPN,
co-author of *Chicken Soup for the Nurse's Soul*

Blessed is the man that trusteth in the LORD, and whose hope the LORD is.   JEREMIAH 17:7

He healeth the broken in heart, and bindeth up their wounds.   PSALM 147:3

And every man that hath this hope in him purifieth himself, even as he is pure.   1 JOHN 3:3

For the hope which is laid up for you in heaven, whereof ye heard before in the word of the truth of the gospel. . .   COLOSSIANS 1:5

Which is Christ in you,

the hope of glory.

COLOSSIANS 1:27

Be of good courage, and he shall strengthen your heart, all ye that hope in the LORD.

PSALM 31:24

For thou art my hope, O Lord GOD: thou art my trust from my youth.   PSALM 71:5

Blessed be the God and Father of our Lord Jesus Christ, which according to his abundant mercy hath begotten us again unto a lively hope by the resurrection of Jesus Christ from the dead.

1 PETER 1:3

And not only so, but we glory in tribulations also: knowing that tribulation worketh patience; and patience, experience; and experience, hope: and hope maketh not ashamed.   ROMANS 5:3–5

The hope of the righteous shall be gladness: but the expectation of the wicked shall perish.
                                                        PROVERBS 10:28

Thou art my hiding place and my shield: I hope in thy word.   PSALM 119:114

My soul fainteth for thy salvation: but I hope in thy word.   PSALM 119:81

Now the God of hope fill you with all joy and peace in believing, that ye may abound in hope, through the power of the Holy Ghost.   ROMANS 15:13

But sanctify the Lord God in your hearts: and be ready always to give an answer to every man that asketh you a reason of the hope that is in you with meekness and fear.   1 PETER 3:15

For we through the Spirit wait for the hope of righteousness by faith.   GALATIANS 5:5

Who by him do believe in God, that raised him up from the dead, and gave him glory; that your faith and hope might be in God.   1 PETER 1:21

And have hope toward God, which they themselves also allow, that there shall be a resurrection of the dead, both of the just and unjust.   ACTS 24:15

But I will hope continually, and will yet praise thee more and more.   PSALM 71:14

There is one body,

and one Spirit,

even as ye are called in

one hope of your calling.

EPHESIANS 4:4

And we desire that every one of you do shew the same diligence to the full assurance of hope unto the end.   HEBREWS 6:11

For we are saved by hope: but hope that is seen is not hope: for what a man seeth, why doth he yet hope for? But if we hope for that we see not, then do we with patience wait for it.   ROMANS 8:24–25

LORD, I have hoped for thy salvation, and done thy commandments.   PSALM 119:166

Therefore, since we have such a hope, we are very bold. 2 CORINTHIANS 3:12 NIV

The eyes of your understanding being enlightened; that ye may know what is the hope of his calling, and what the riches of the glory of his inheritance in the saints. EPHESIANS 1:18

Remember the word unto thy servant, upon which thou hast caused me to hope. PSALM 119:49

For the hope which is laid up for you in heaven, whereof ye heard before in the word of the truth of the gospel. COLOSSIANS 1:5

Looking for that blessed hope, and the glorious appearing of the great God and our Saviour Jesus Christ. TITUS 2:13

When life's light dims, when things are overwhelming, Father, set a torch in my hand. Strengthen me so I can lift high Your beacon of hope. Let Your promises shine so the path isn't so dark and lonely. Walk beside me and whisper Your promises and comfort. Let me recall the mighty times when You've proven Yourself, and imbue me with faith so I can believe whatever lies ahead is good, because I will still be in Your hands. Amen.

A nurse's heart is a servant's heart from birth to death with those she cares for.

GENEVIEVE O'BRIEN, RN

We know that our body—the tent we live in here on earth—will be destroyed. But when that happens, God will have a house for us. It will not be a house made by human hands; instead, it will be a home in heaven that will last forever.

2 CORINTHIANS 5:1 NCV

How amiable are thy tabernacles, O LORD of hosts! My soul longeth, yea, even fainteth for the courts of the LORD: my heart and my flesh crieth out for the living God. PSALM 84:1–2

Our physical body is becoming older and weaker, but our spirit inside us is made new every day. We have small troubles for a while now, but they are helping us gain an eternal glory that is much greater than the troubles. We set our eyes not on what we see but on what we cannot see. What we see will last only a short time, but what we cannot see will last forever. 2 Corinthians 4:16–18 NCV

Remember your Creator while you are young, before the days of trouble come and the years when you say, "I find no pleasure in them." When you get old, the light from the sun, moon, and stars will grow dark; the rain clouds will never seem to go away. At that time your arms will shake and your legs will become weak. Your teeth will fall out so that you cannot chew, and your eyes will not see clearly. Your ears will be deaf to the noise in the streets, and you will barely hear the millstone grinding grain. You'll wake up when a bird starts singing, but you will barely hear singing. You will fear high places and will be afraid to go for a walk. Your hair will become white like the flowers on an almond tree. You will limp along like a grasshopper when you walk. Your appetite will be gone. Then you will go to your everlasting home, and people will go to your funeral. . . . You will turn back into the dust of the earth again, but your spirit will return to God who gave it. Ecclesiastes 12:1–5, 7 NCV

Oh, the quiet comfort that You bring, Lord. How thankful I am for the moments when You are beside me and make Yourself known. Healing is not just a recovery from illness—it is the completion of a life, the fullness of a soul, the submission to eternity with the faith that better things lie ahead. Help me to let go with grace, to rely on faith, and know You are the King of yesterday's memories, the Lord of today's challenges, and the Keeper of eternity. Amen.

HUMILITY

The King of kings washed feet and touched lepers. He is our example. Nursing isn't about glamour or glory. You give of yourself in thousands of fundamental, essential ways because someone requires your care.

CATHY HAKE, RN

When men are cast down, then thou shalt say, There is lifting up; and he shall save the humble person. JOB 22:29

And whosoever shall exalt himself shall be abased; and he that shall humble himself shall be exalted. MATTHEW 23:12

Whosoever therefore shall humble himself as this little child, the same is greatest in the kingdom of heaven. MATTHEW 18:4

By humility and the fear of the LORD are riches, and honour, and life.   PROVERBS 22:4

Better it is to be of an humble spirit with the lowly, than to divide the spoil with the proud.
                                        PROVERBS 16:19

The fear of the LORD is

the instruction of wisdom;

and before honour is humility.

PROVERBS 15:33

But he giveth more grace. Wherefore he saith, God resisteth the proud, but giveth grace unto the humble.   JAMES 4:6

For I say, through the grace given unto me, to every man that is among you, not to think of himself more highly than he ought to think; but to think soberly, according as God hath dealt to every man the measure of faith.   ROMANS 12:3

A man's pride shall bring him low: but honour shall uphold the humble in spirit.   PROVERBS 29:23

Humble yourselves therefore under the mighty hand of God, that he may exalt you in due time.

1 PETER 5:6

Let another man praise thee, and not thine own mouth; a stranger, and not thine own lips.

PROVERBS 27:2

Boast not thyself of to morrow; for thou knowest not what a day may bring forth.   PROVERBS 27:1

Blessed are the poor in spirit: for theirs is the kingdom of heaven.   MATTHEW 5:3

LORD, thou hast heard the desire of the humble: thou wilt prepare their heart, thou wilt cause thine ear to hear.   PSALM 10:17

It's not about me, God. Help me to remember that. Christ, the King, came as a servant. I want to be like Him. Cultivate a servant's heart in me. Teach me to set aside myself and seek to put the needs of others first. Let me strive for the welfare of my brothers and sisters. Your Son washed feet, and that thought humbles me. My hands—Father, here are my knees and hands. Show me where to kneel, what to touch and tend in Your name. Amen.

I am blessed that I am a nurse and can be there for very sick people in a very vulnerable time. I have found that the Lord works in such wonderful ways. It definitely helps to be a nurse who is very secure in her beliefs.

HEATHER WIERACHS, RN, BSN,
CARDIOTHORACIC SURGICAL

Keep thy heart with all diligence; for out of it are the issues of life.   PROVERBS 4:23

In whose hand is the soul of every living thing, and the breath of all mankind.   JOB 12:10

O LORD, by these things men live, and in all these things is the life of my spirit: so wilt thou recover me, and make me to live.   ISAIAH 38:16

Beloved, I do not consider that I have made it my own, but this is one thing I do: forgetting what lies behind and straining forward to what lies ahead, I press on toward the goal for the prize of the heavenly call of God in Christ Jesus.

PHILIPPIANS 3:13-14 NRSV

For I will restore health unto thee, and I will heal thee of thy wounds.

JEREMIAH 30:17

All praise to the God and Father of our Lord Jesus Christ. He is the source of every mercy and the God who comforts us. He comforts us in all our troubles so that we can comfort others. When others are troubled, we will be able to give them the same comfort God has given us.

2 CORINTHIANS 1:3–4 NLT

The LORD is my portion, saith my soul; therefore will I hope in him. The LORD is good unto them that wait for him, to the soul that seeketh him. It is good that a man should both hope and quietly wait for the salvation of the LORD.

LAMENTATIONS 3:24–26

But You, O GOD, the Lord, deal kindly with me for Your name's sake; because Your lovingkindness is good, deliver me; for I am afflicted and needy, and my heart is wounded within me. I am passing like a shadow when it lengthens.

PSALM 109:21–23 NAS

Come, see the glorious things God has done. What marvelous miracles happen to his people!
PSALM 66:5 TLB

But though he cause grief, yet will he have compassion according to the multitude of his mercies. For he doth not afflict willingly nor grieve the children of men. LAMENTATIONS 3:32–33

Heal me, O LORD, and I shall be healed; save me, and I shall be saved: for thou art my praise.
JEREMIAH 17:14

Behold, I have refined thee, but not with silver; I have chosen thee in the furnace of affliction.
ISAIAH 48:10

The ventilator oxygenates lungs, but You breathe the breath of life into each living soul. All-powerful Father, You made man's body to be such a magnificent creation—but my patients are so very sick and broken. Hearts and lives are in the balance, Father. Each minute, each decision matters. Help me look past the machinery and tubes, beyond the medications, and touch the patients. Minister through me to heal them in Your name, but if the time comes that You call them home, give me grace to let go. Amen.

JOY

*L ive your life while you have it. Life is a splendid gift—
there is nothing small about it.*

FLORENCE NIGHTINGALE

Joy is a net of love by which you can catch souls.

MOTHER TERESA

For ye shall go out with joy, and be led forth with peace: the mountains and the hills shall break forth before you into singing, and all the trees of the field shall clap their hands.　　ISAIAH 55:12

These things have I spoken unto you, that my joy might remain in you, and that your joy might be full.　　JOHN 15:11

Blessed is the people that know the joyful sound: they shall walk, O LORD, in the light of thy countenance. In thy name shall they rejoice all the day: and in thy righteousness shall they be exalted.

PSALM 89:15–16

The LORD is my strength and my shield; my heart trusted in him, and I am helped: therefore my heart greatly rejoiceth; and with my song will I praise him.

PSALM 28:7

Light is sown for the righteous, and gladness for the upright in heart. Rejoice in the LORD, ye righteous; and give thanks at the remembrance of his holiness.

PSALM 97:11–12

Yet I will rejoice in the LORD, I will joy in the God of my salvation.

HABAKKUK 3:18

For our heart shall rejoice in him, because we have trusted in his holy name.

PSALM 33:21

For then shalt thou have thy delight in the Almighty, and shalt lift up thy face unto God.

JOB 22:26

Whom having not seen, ye love; in whom, though now ye see him not, yet believing, ye rejoice with joy unspeakable and full of glory.

1 PETER 1:8

And thou shalt rejoice in the LORD, and shalt glory in the Holy One of Israel.   ISAIAH 41:16

The righteous shall be glad in the LORD, and shall trust in him; and all the upright in heart shall glory.   PSALM 64:10

My soul shall be satisfied as with marrow and fatness; and my mouth shall praise thee with joyful lips.   PSALM 63:5

Rejoice in the Lord alway:

and again I say, Rejoice.

PHILIPPIANS 4:4

But let the righteous be glad; let them rejoice before God: yea, let them exceedingly rejoice.

PSALM 68:3

Hitherto have ye asked nothing in my name: ask, and ye shall receive, that your joy may be full.

JOHN 16:24

Be glad in the LORD, and rejoice, ye righteous: and shout for joy, all ye that are upright in heart.

PSALM 32:11

I will see you again, and your heart shall rejoice, and your joy no man taketh from you.   JOHN 16:22

My lips shall greatly rejoice when I sing unto thee; and my soul, which thou hast redeemed.
                                                    PSALM 71:23

A merry heart doeth good like a medicine.
                                                    PROVERBS 17:22

Make a joyful noise unto the LORD, all ye lands. Serve the LORD with gladness: come before his presence with singing.   PSALM 100:1–2

Let all those that seek thee rejoice and be glad in thee: let such as love thy salvation say continually, The LORD be magnified.   PSALM 40:16

Speaking to yourselves in psalms and hymns and spiritual songs, singing and making melody in your heart to the Lord.   EPHESIANS 5:19

Father, how can I be other than joyful? I am Your child and live in Your presence. Let me be ever mindful of the wonders that surround me, things large and small that echo Your love and might. Amen.

LONELINESS

You see a lot of lonely people in your nursing practice. They have empty places in their hearts—and you can fill them just as God fills those places in your life.

ELVERA SMITH, RN

I will not leave you comfortless: I will come to you.

JOHN 14:18

Then shalt thou call, and the LORD shall answer; thou shalt cry, and he shall say, Here I am.

ISAIAH 58:9

Yet the LORD will command his lovingkindness in the day time, and in the night his song shall be with me, and my prayer unto the God of my life.

PSALM 42:8

Since thou wast precious in my sight, thou hast been honourable, and I have loved thee. ISAIAH 43:4

And will be a Father unto you, and ye shall be my sons and daughters, saith the Lord Almighty.
2 CORINTHIANS 6:18

And, behold, I am with thee, and will keep thee in all places whither thou goest, and will bring thee again into this land; for I will not leave thee, until I have done that which I have spoken to thee of.
GENESIS 28:15

I will praise the LORD, who counsels me; even at night my heart instructs me. I have set the LORD always before me. Because he is at my right hand, I will not be shaken. PSALM 16:7–8 NIV

Sometimes, even in the midst of a crowd, I feel so alone, Lord. You make Your presence known to me in so many ways—and Your Word is full of promises that You will never leave or forsake me. Teach me to hold on to the promises in the midst of the crowd and in the darkness of night. Bless me with Your presence so that I might go out and encourage others who also seek to know the joy of Your overwhelming love. Amen.

I can't imagine being a nurse without loving God, because nursing is really showing God's love. It is a vocation—answering a spiritual call and being in the center of His will. Loving Him allows me the opportunity to care for others.

DOTTIE CRUMMY, PH.D.,
CHAIR OF NURSING DEPARTMENT,
POINT LOMA NAZARENE UNIVERSITY

And thou shalt love the LORD thy God with all thine heart, and with all thy soul, and with all thy might.   DEUTERONOMY 6:5

I love them that love me; and those that seek me early shall find me.   PROVERBS 8:17

Delight thyself also in the LORD: and he shall give thee the desires of thine heart.   PSALM 37:4

Because he hath set his love upon me, therefore will I deliver him: I will set him on high, because he hath known my name.   PSALM 91:14

But as it is written, Eye hath not seen, nor ear heard, neither have entered into the heart of man, the things which God hath prepared for them that love him.   1 CORINTHIANS 2:9

The LORD preserveth all them that love him: but all the wicked will he destroy.   PSALM 145:20

Grace be with all them that love our Lord Jesus Christ in sincerity.   EPHESIANS 6:24

The LORD preserveth

all them that love him.

PSALM 145:20

Take good heed therefore unto yourselves, that ye love the LORD your God.   JOSHUA 23:11

But if any man love God, the same is known of him.   1 CORINTHIANS 8:3

Keep yourselves in the love of God, looking for the mercy of our Lord Jesus Christ unto eternal life.

JUDE 21

Jesus said unto them, If God were your Father, ye would love me: for I proceeded forth and came from God; neither came I of myself, but he sent me.   JOHN 8:42

Love not the world, neither the things that are in the world. If any man love the world, the love of the Father is not in him.   1 JOHN 2:15

My son, give me thine heart, and let thine eyes observe my ways.   PROVERBS 23:26

What a joy it is to sing Your praises, to kneel in Your presence, to live in Your shadow. You teach me what love is—I want to reflect back the fullness of my heart and soul to You. Amen.

In a world where there is so much to be done, I felt strongly impressed that there must be something for me to do.
DOROTHEA DIX

This thing is too much for you; you are not able to perform it by yourself.   EXODUS 18:18 NKJV

I will bless the Lord who counsels me; he gives me wisdom in the night. He tells me what to do.
PSALM 16:7 TLB

He nurses them when they are sick, and soothes their pains and worries.   PSALM 41:3 TLB

The Lord is close to those whose hearts are breaking.   PSALM 34:18 TLB

Trust the Lord completely; don't ever trust yourself. In everything you do, put God first, and he will direct you and crown your efforts with success.

PROVERBS 3:5 TLB

Now Isaiah had said, "Let them take a cake of figs and apply it to the boil, that he may recover."

ISAIAH 38:21 NAS

And heal the sick that are therein, and say unto them, The kingdom of God is come nigh unto you.

LUKE 10:9

And went to him,

and bound up his wounds,

pouring in oil and wine. . .

and took care of him.

LUKE 10:34

But thou, O Lord, art a God full of compassion, and gracious, longsuffering, and plenteous in mercy and truth.   PSALM 86:15

I was eyes to the blind, and feet was I to the lame.

JOB 29:15

And make straight paths for your feet, so that the limb which is lame may not be put out of joint, but rather be healed.　　　　HEBREWS 12:13 NAS

And Simon's wife's mother was taken with a great fever; and they besought him for her. And he stood over her, and rebuked the fever; and it left her: and immediately she arose and ministered unto them.

LUKE 4:38–39

Now when the sun was setting, all they that had any sick with divers diseases brought them unto him; and he laid his hands on every one of them, and healed them.　　　　LUKE 4:40

Publius' father was sick with a fever and dysentery. Paul went to him, prayed, and put his hands on the man and healed him.　　　　ACTS 28:8 NCV

Wherefore the rather, brethren, give diligence to make your calling and election sure: for if ye do these things, ye shall never fall: for so an entrance shall be ministered unto you abundantly into the everlasting kingdom of our Lord and Saviour Jesus Christ.　　　　2 PETER 1:10–11

Why is my pain perpetual, and my wound incurable, which refuseth to be healed? . . . I am with thee to save thee and to deliver thee, saith the LORD.　　　　JEREMIAH 15:18, 20

He hath made his wonderful works to be remembered: the LORD is gracious and full of compassion.
PSALM 111:4

Look upon mine affliction and my pain; and forgive all my sins. PSALM 25:18

Unto the upright there ariseth light in the darkness: he is gracious, and full of compassion, and righteous. PSALM 112:4

Have mercy upon me, O LORD; for I am weak: O LORD, heal me; for my bones are vexed.
PSALM 6:2

My knees are weak from fasting, and my flesh has grown lean, without fatness. . . . Help me, O LORD my God; save me according to Your lovingkindness. And let them know that this is Your hand; You, LORD, have done it. PSALM 109:24, 26–27 NAS

He delivereth the poor in his affliction, and openeth their ears in oppression. JOB 36:15

This is my comfort in my affliction: for thy word hath quickened me. PSALM 119:50

What do ye imagine against the LORD? he will make an utter end: affliction shall not rise up the second time. NAHUM 1:9

O LORD, my strength, and my fortress, and my refuge in the day of affliction.   JEREMIAH 16:19

There shall no evil befall thee, neither shall any plague come nigh thy dwelling.   PSALM 91:10

And Moses cried unto the LORD, saying, Heal her now, O God, I beseech thee.   NUMBERS 12:13

For I will restore health unto thee,

and I will heal thee

of thy wounds.

JEREMIAH 30:17

I have seen his ways, and will heal him: I will lead him also, and restore comforts unto him and to his mourners. . .saith the LORD; and I will heal him.
ISAIAH 57:18–19

Heal the sick, cleanse the lepers, raise the dead, cast out devils: freely ye have received, freely give.
MATTHEW 10:8

And he sent them to preach the kingdom of God, and to heal the sick.   LUKE 9:2

That they should be with him, and that he might send them forth. . .to have power to heal.

MARK 3:14–15

I'm juggling, God. Doctors' orders, patients' needs, medication schedules, treatments, charting. . . I wanted to be a nurse so I could care. Please, Father, help me care—physically, spiritually, and emotionally for my patients today. Amen.

You must never so much as think whether you like it or not, whether it is bearable or not; you must never think of anything except the need, and how to meet it.

CLARA BARTON

And now abideth faith, hope, charity, these three; but the greatest of these is charity.

1 CORINTHIANS 13:13

Rejoice with them that do rejoice, and weep with them that weep.

ROMANS 12:15

Be ye therefore merciful, as your Father also is merciful.

LUKE 6:36

The LORD is good to all: and his tender mercies are over all his works.

PSALM 145:9

Therefore turn thou to thy God: keep mercy and judgment and wait on thy God continually.

HOSEA 12:6

Let not mercy and truth forsake thee: bind them about thy neck; write them upon the table of thine heart: so shalt thou find favour and good understanding in the sight of God and man.

PROVERBS 3:3–4

Or he that exhorteth, on exhortation: he that giveth, let him do it with simplicity; he that ruleth, with diligence; he that sheweth mercy, with cheerfulness.

ROMANS 12:8

Blessed are the merciful:

for they shall obtain mercy.

MATTHEW 5:7

Above all things have fervent charity among yourselves: for charity shall cover the multitude of sins. Use hospitality one to another without grudging. As every man hath received the gift, even so minister the same one to another, as good stewards of the manifold grace of God.   1 PETER 4:8–10

As we have therefore opportunity, let us do good unto all men, especially unto them who are of the household of faith.   GALATIANS 6:10

And if thou draw out thy soul to the hungry, and satisfy the afflicted soul; then shall thy light rise in obscurity, and thy darkness be as the noon day.
                                        ISAIAH 58:10

It is of the LORD's mercies that we are not consumed, because his compassions fail not. They are new every morning: great is thy faithfulness.
                                  LAMENTATIONS 3:22–23

Create in me a compassionate heart, Lord. Open my eyes to the needs of others. Blind me to the selfishness that would hold me back from tending others in Your name. Clothe me in Your mercy and fill my heart with empathy. Use me, my hands, my words, to be Your love in action. Amen.

OBEDIENCE

Through our obedience to the Holy Spirit, we are empowered to give consistent, Christian caring.
REBEKAH FLEEGER, CHAIR, DEPARTMENT OF
BACCALAUREATE NURSING, BIOLA UNIVERSITY

Blessed are they that keep his testimonies, and that seek him with the whole heart.   PSALM 119:2

Now therefore, if ye will obey my voice indeed, and keep my covenant, then ye shall be a peculiar treasure unto me above all people: for all the earth is mine.   EXODUS 19:5

If ye keep my commandments, ye shall abide in my love; even as I have kept my Father's commandments, and abide in his love.   JOHN 15:10

Thou shalt keep therefore his statutes, and his commandments, which I command thee this day, that it may go well with thee, and with thy children after thee, and that thou mayest prolong thy days upon the earth, which the LORD thy God giveth thee, for ever.   DEUTERONOMY 4:40

And thou shalt do that which is right and good in the sight of the LORD: that it may be well with thee.   DEUTERONOMY 6:18

See, I have set before thee this day life and good, and death and evil; in that I command thee this day to love the LORD thy God, to walk in his ways, and to keep his commandments and his statutes and his judgments, that thou mayest live and multiply: and the LORD thy God shall bless thee in the land whither thou goest to possess it.
                    DEUTERONOMY 30:15–16

Hear therefore, O Israel, and observe to do it; that it may be well with thee, and that ye may increase mightily, as the LORD God of thy fathers hath promised thee, in the land that floweth with milk and honey.   DEUTERONOMY 6:3

Wherefore it shall come to pass, if ye hearken to these judgments, and keep, and do them, that the LORD thy God shall keep unto thee the covenant and the mercy which he sware unto thy fathers.
                    DEUTERONOMY 7:12

Keep therefore the words of this covenant, and do them, that ye may prosper in all that ye do.

DEUTERONOMY 29:9

O that there were such an heart in them, that they would fear me, and keep all my commandments always, that it might be well with them, and with their children for ever! DEUTERONOMY 5:29

But he said, Yea rather,

blessed are they that hear

the word of God, and keep it.

LUKE 11:28

Those things, which ye have both learned, and received, and heard, and seen in me, do: and the God of peace shall be with you. PHILIPPIANS 4:9

For whosoever shall do the will of my Father which is in heaven, the same is my brother, and sister, and mother. MATTHEW 12:50

And the world passeth away, and the lust thereof: but he that doeth the will of God abideth for ever.

1 JOHN 2:17

Whosoever therefore shall break one of these least commandments, and shall teach men so, he shall be called the least in the kingdom of heaven: but whosoever shall do and teach them, the same shall be called great in the kingdom of heaven.

MATTHEW 5:19

Therefore whosoever heareth these sayings of mine, and doeth them, I will liken him unto a wise man, which built his house upon a rock: and the rain descended, and the floods came, and the winds blew, and beat upon that house; and it fell not: for it was founded upon a rock.   MATTHEW 7:24–25

If they obey and serve him, they shall spend their days in prosperity, and their years in pleasures.

JOB 36:11

But whoso looketh into the perfect law of liberty, and continueth therein, he being not a forgetful hearer, but a doer of the work, this man shall be blessed in his deed.   JAMES 1:25

Not every one that saith unto me, Lord, Lord, shall enter into the kingdom of heaven; but he that doeth the will of my Father which is in heaven.

MATTHEW 7:21

And whatsoever we ask, we receive of him, because we keep his commandments, and do those things that are pleasing in his sight.   1 JOHN 3:22

Observe and hear all these words which I command thee, that it may go well with thee, and with thy children after thee for ever, when thou doest that which is good and right in the sight of the LORD thy God.   DEUTERONOMY 12:28

My son, forget not my law; but let thine heart keep my commandments: for length of days, and long life, and peace, shall they add to thee.
                                                           PROVERBS 3:1–2

All the paths of the LORD are mercy and truth unto such as keep his covenant and his testimonies.
                                                                PSALM 25:10

If ye be willing and obedient, ye shall eat the good of the land.   ISAIAH 1:19

Let us hear the conclusion of the whole matter: Fear God, and keep his commandments: for this is the whole duty of man.   ECCLESIASTES 12:13

I'm a stiff-necked, headstrong child, Father. In my stubbornness, I want to do things my way. It's so easy to charge ahead rather than to seek Your will. Attune my ear to Your voice, and teach me to listen and obey. Amen.

There is nothing like the miracle of a woman carrying a child. The progression from conception to birth is all because of God's divine design.

MARILYN WHITEHEAD, RNP, OBSTETRICS

Lo, children are an heritage of the LORD: and the fruit of the womb is his reward. As arrows are in the hand of a mighty man; so are children of the youth. Happy is the man that hath his quiver full of them: they shall not be ashamed, but they shall speak with the enemies in the gate.   PSALM 127:3–5

But thou art he that took me out of the womb: thou didst make me hope when I was upon my mother's breasts. I was cast upon thee from the womb: thou art my God from my mother's belly.

PSALM 22:9–10

Thy wife shall be as a fruitful vine by the sides of thine house: thy children like olive plants round about thy table. PSALM 128:3

A woman when she is in travail hath sorrow, because her hour is come: but as soon as she is delivered of the child, she remembereth no more the anguish, for joy that a man is born into the world. JOHN 16:21

He gives children to the woman

who has none

and makes her a happy mother.

PSALM 113:9 NCV

You made my whole being; you formed me in my mother's body. I praise you because you made me in an amazing and wonderful way. What you have done is wonderful. I know this very well. You saw my bones being formed as I took shape in my mother's body. When I was put together there, you saw my body as it was formed. All the days planned for me were written in your book before I was one day old. PSALM 139:13–16 NCV

138

He shall feed his flock like a shepherd: he shall gather the lambs with his arm, and carry them in his bosom, and shall gently lead those that are with young.   ISAIAH 40:11

Through faith also Sara herself received strength to conceive seed, and was delivered of a child when she was past age, because she judged him faithful who had promised.   HEBREWS 11:11

As you do not know the path of the wind, or how the body is formed in a mother's womb, so you cannot understand the work of God, the Maker of all things.   ECCLESIASTES 11:5 NIV

Merciful Father, giver of life, I stand in awe each time a woman conceives, carries a baby, and gives birth. This miracle wears Your name, Your genius, Your love. For months, You have woven life and instilled a soul. Help me to foster that flicker of life, to respect it, to honor Your gift of creation. Help me to give comfort to this mother, to reassure her husband, to securely hold the new baby. Let me bear witness to Your greatness, to speak of the wonders You bring forth, and hear my thanks for allowing me to be present as You breathe that first breath of life into each baby. Amen.

A ll things pass. . . .
Patience attains all it strives for.

MOTHER TERESA

Wait on the LORD: be of good courage, and he shall strengthen thine heart: wait, I say, on the LORD.

PSALM 27:14

For what glory is it, if, when ye be buffeted for your faults, ye shall take it patiently? but if, when ye do well, and suffer for it, ye take it patiently, this is acceptable with God.   1 PETER 2:20

That ye be not slothful, but followers of them who through faith and patience inherit the promises.

HEBREWS 6:12

Let us hold fast the profession of our faith without wavering. HEBREWS 10:23

But he that shall endure unto the end, the same shall be saved. MATTHEW 24:13

For ye have need of patience, that, after ye have done the will of God, ye might receive the promise. HEBREWS 10:36

My brethren, count it all joy when ye fall into divers temptations; knowing this, that the trying of your faith worketh patience. But let patience have her perfect work, that ye may be perfect and entire, wanting nothing. JAMES 1:2–4

Be sober, grave, temperate, sound in faith, in charity, in patience. TITUS 2:2

And not only so, but we glory in tribulations also: knowing that tribulation worketh patience; and patience, experience; and experience, hope. ROMANS 5:3–4

But that on the good ground are they, which in an honest and good heart, having heard the word, keep it, and bring forth fruit with patience. LUKE 8:15

But in all things approving ourselves as the ministers of God, in much patience, in afflictions, in necessities, in distresses. 2 CORINTHIANS 6:4

Rest in the LORD, and wait patiently for him: fret not thyself because of him who prospereth in his way, because of the man who bringeth wicked devices to pass. Cease from anger, and forsake wrath: fret not thyself in any wise to do evil. For evildoers shall be cut off: but those that wait upon the LORD, they shall inherit the earth.

PSALM 37:7–9

And the servant of the Lord

must not strive;

but be gentle unto all men,

apt to teach, patient.

2 TIMOTHY 2:24

For whatsoever things were written aforetime were written for our learning, that we through patience and comfort of the scriptures might have hope. Now the God of patience and consolation grant you to be likeminded one toward another according to Christ Jesus.   ROMANS 15:4–5

And so, after he had patiently endured, he obtained the promise.   HEBREWS 6:15

And the Lord direct your hearts into the love of God, and into the patient waiting for Christ.

2 THESSALONIANS 3:5

Wherefore seeing we also are compassed about with so great a cloud of witnesses, let us lay aside every weight, and the sin which doth so easily beset us, and let us run with patience the race that is set before us.   HEBREWS 12:1

Better is the end of a thing than the beginning thereof: and the patient in spirit is better than the proud in spirit.   ECCLESIASTES 7:8

To them who by patient continuance in well doing seek for glory and honour and immortality, eternal life.   ROMANS 2:7

I'm pressed for time, Father. There's so much to do, but not enough of me to go around. Waiting on anything seems like an impossibility, but it's wrong to hurry someone weak to walk or chew faster. Enduring while anticipating what lies ahead—spiritually, professionally, personally—is so hard. While I wait, help me to find a still spot in my soul and know that You are God. Amen.

I've decided that peace isn't living a trouble-free life that has no tensions or struggles; it's resting in God's presence in the midst of all that is going on.

CATHY HAKE, RN

Peace, peace to him that is far off, and to him that is near, saith the LORD; and I will heal him.

ISAIAH 57:19

And let the peace of God rule in your hearts, to the which also ye are called in one body; and be ye thankful.

COLOSSIANS 3:15

I will hear what God the LORD will speak: for he will speak peace unto his people, and to his saints.

PSALM 85:8

And the work of righteousness shall be peace; and the effect of righteousness quietness and assurance for ever. ISAIAH 32:17

Mark the perfect man, and behold the upright: for the end of that man is peace. PSALM 37:37

Now the Lord of peace himself give you peace always by all means. 2 THESSALONIANS 3:16

Now the God of hope fill you with all joy and peace in believing, that ye may abound in hope, through the power of the Holy Ghost. ROMANS 15:13

I exhort therefore, that, first of all, supplications, prayers, intercessions, and giving of thanks, be made for all men; for kings, and for all that are in authority; that we may lead a quiet and peaceable life in all godliness and honesty. 1 TIMOTHY 2:1–2

Blessed are the peacemakers: for they shall be called the children of God. MATTHEW 5:9

The LORD will give strength unto his people; the LORD will bless his people with peace.
PSALM 29:11

And the peace of God, which passeth all understanding, shall keep your hearts and minds through Christ Jesus. PHILIPPIANS 4:7

Deceit is in the heart of them that imagine evil: but to the counsellors of peace is joy.   PROVERBS 12:20

And the fruit of righteousness is sown in peace of them that make peace.   JAMES 3:18

Endeavouring to keep the unity of the Spirit in the bond of peace.   EPHESIANS 4:3

If it be possible, as much as lieth in you, live peaceably with all men.   ROMANS 12:18

Thy faith hath saved thee;

go in peace.

LUKE 7:50

And to esteem them very highly in love for their work's sake. And be at peace among yourselves.
1 THESSALONIANS 5:13

Follow peace with all men, and holiness, without which no man shall see the Lord.   HEBREWS 12:14

For God hath not given us the spirit of fear; but of power, and of love, and of a sound mind.
2 TIMOTHY 1:7

Behold, how good and how pleasant it is for brethren to dwell together in unity!   PSALM 133:1

For he that will love life, and see good days, let him refrain his tongue from evil, and his lips that they speak no guile: let him eschew evil, and do good; let him seek peace, and ensue it.   1 PETER 3:10–11

Thou wilt keep him in perfect peace, whose mind is stayed on thee: because he trusteth in thee.

ISAIAH 26:3

Peace I leave with you, my peace I give unto you: not as the world giveth, give I unto you. Let not your heart be troubled, neither let it be afraid.

JOHN 14:27

Lord, You know what troubles my heart today. The clamor all around me distracts me and makes it difficult to find a moment of rest from the turmoil. Even now, in a quiet place, my mind races, trying to find a solution. Father, I seek Your perfect peace. You promise that I can cast all my cares on You and rest in You. Help me to let go of the things I can do nothing to change. Give me wisdom to move forward where I can make a difference. Thank You, Lord, for Your promise to give me peace. Amen.

A few hours will do for baby, both in killing and curing it, what days will not do for a grown-up person.

FLORENCE NIGHTINGALE

But when Jesus saw it, he was much displeased, and said unto them, Suffer the little children to come unto me, and forbid them not: for of such is the kingdom of God. Verily I say unto you, Whosoever shall not receive the kingdom of God as a little child, he shall not enter therein. And he took them up in his arms, put his hands upon them, and blessed them.   MARK 10:14–16

And all thy children shall be taught of the LORD; and great shall be the peace of thy children.

ISAIAH 54:13

When thou liest down, thou shalt not be afraid: yea, thou shalt lie down, and thy sleep shall be sweet.

PROVERBS 3:24

You welcomed the little ones to come unto You, Jesus. As I care for Your lambs, give me an extra measure of tenderness and compassion. Free them from fear and restore them, I pray. Amen.

I have an almost complete disregard of precedent and a faith in the possibility of something better. It irritates me to be told how things always have been done. . . . I defy the tyranny of precedent. I cannot afford the luxury of a closed mind. I go for anything new that might improve the past.

CLARA BARTON,
from *A Chosen Faith*

When times are good, be happy; but when times are bad, consider: God has made the one as well as the other.   ECCLESIASTES 7:14 NIV

Behold, we count them happy which endure. Ye have heard of the patience of Job, and have seen the end of the Lord; that the Lord is very pitiful, and of tender mercy.   JAMES 5:11

For the which cause I also suffer these things: nevertheless I am not ashamed: for I know whom I have believed, and am persuaded that he is able to keep that which I have committed unto him against that day. Hold fast the form of sound words, which thou hast heard of me, in faith and love which is in Christ Jesus.   2 TIMOTHY 1:12–13

He that hath an ear, let him hear what the Spirit saith unto the churches; He that overcometh shall not be hurt of the second death.

REVELATION 2:11

For we are made partakers of Christ, if we hold the beginning of our confidence stedfast unto the end.

HEBREWS 3:14

To him that overcometh will I grant to sit with me in my throne, even as I also overcame, and am set down with my Father in his throne.

REVELATION 3:21

That the trial of your faith, being much more precious than of gold that perisheth, though it be tried with fire, might be found unto praise and honour and glory at the appearing of Jesus Christ.

1 PETER 1:7

Thou therefore endure hardness, as a good soldier of Jesus Christ.   2 TIMOTHY 2:3

Praying always with all prayer and supplication in the Spirit, and watching thereunto with all perseverance and supplication for all saints.

EPHESIANS 6:18

Teaching us that, denying ungodliness and worldly lusts, we should live soberly, righteously, and godly, in this present world; looking for that blessed hope, and the glorious appearing of the great God and our Saviour Jesus Christ.

TITUS 2:12–13

Let us hold fast the profession of our faith without wavering; (for he is faithful that promised).

HEBREWS 10:23

Though he fall, he shall not be utterly cast down: for the LORD upholdeth him with his hand.

PSALM 37:24

Stand fast therefore in the liberty wherewith Christ hath made us free, and be not entangled again with the yoke of bondage.

GALATIANS 5:1

But ye, brethren, be not weary in well doing.
2 THESSALONIANS 3:13

For I am persuaded, that neither death, nor life, nor angels, nor principalities, nor powers, nor things present, nor things to come, nor height, nor depth, nor any other creature, shall be able to separate us from the love of God, which is in Christ Jesus our Lord.
ROMANS 8:38–39

But the path of the just is as the shining light, that shineth more and more unto the perfect day.
PROVERBS 4:18

Then said Jesus to those Jews which believed on him, If ye continue in my word, then are ye my disciples indeed.
JOHN 8:31

Ye therefore, beloved, seeing ye know these things before, beware lest ye also, being led away with the error of the wicked, fall from your own stedfastness.
2 PETER 3:17

For now we live, if ye stand fast in the Lord.
1 THESSALONIANS 3:8

Confirming the souls of the disciples, and exhorting them to continue in the faith, and that we must through much tribulation enter into the kingdom of God.
ACTS 14:22

Who shall separate us from the love of Christ? shall tribulation, or distress, or persecution, or famine, or nakedness, or peril, or sword?   ROMANS 8:35

Wherefore take unto you the whole armour of God, that ye may be able to withstand in the evil day, and having done all, to stand.   EPHESIANS 6:13

And let us not be weary in well doing: for in due season we shall reap, if we faint not. GALATIANS 6:9

Wherefore seeing we also are compassed about with so great a cloud of witnesses, let us lay aside every weight, and the sin which doth so easily beset us, and let us run with patience the race that is set before us, looking unto Jesus the author and finisher of our faith; who for the joy that was set before him endured the cross, despising the shame, and is set down at the right hand of the throne of God.   HEBREWS 12:1–2

Therefore, my brethren dearly beloved and longed for, my joy and crown, so stand fast in the Lord, my dearly beloved.   PHILIPPIANS 4:1

Give me a stalwart spirit, Almighty God. Make me resolute in pursuing what is good and right. Help me to chart the right path and keep my feet firmly planted so I can serve Your purpose for me. Amen.

E conomy, prudence, and a simple life are the sure masters
of need, and will often accomplish that which, their op-
posites, with a fortune at hand, will fail to do.

CLARA BARTON

Second Corinthians 2:14 RSV says : "But thanks be to God,
who in Christ always leads us in triumph, and through us
spreads the fragrance of the knowledge of him everywhere."
We are the fragrance of Christ, given the ministry to manifest His presence, grace, compassion, caring, and to be advo-
cates for those in need.

REBEKAH FLEEGER, CHAIR,
DEPARTMENT OF BACCALAUREATE NURSING,
BIOLA UNIVERSITY

Now the end of the commandment is charity out of a pure heart, and of a good conscience, and of faith unfeigned.   1 TIMOTHY 1:5

He that hath mercy on the poor, happy is he.
PROVERBS 14:21

Happy are those who respect the Lord, who want what he commands. . . . They give freely to the poor. The things they do are right and will continue forever. They will be given great honor.
PSALM 112:1, 9 NCV

He raiseth up the poor

out of the dust,

and lifteth the needy

out of the dunghill.

PSALM 113:7

For he shall deliver the needy when he crieth; the poor also, and him that hath no helper. He shall spare the poor and needy, and shall save the souls of the needy.   PSALM 72:12–13

Yet setteth he the poor on high from affliction, and maketh him families like a flock.   PSALM 107:41

For the LORD heareth the poor, and despiseth not his prisoners.   PSALM 69:33

I have shewed you all things, how that so labouring ye ought to support the weak, and to remember the words of the Lord Jesus, how he said, It is more blessed to give than to receive.   ACTS 20:35

Sing unto the LORD, praise ye the LORD: for he hath delivered the soul of the poor from the hand of evildoers.   JEREMIAH 20:13

For the needy shall not alway be forgotten: the expectation of the poor shall not perish for ever.
     PSALM 9:18

But my God shall supply all your need according to his riches in glory by Christ Jesus.
     PHILIPPIANS 4:19

For the poor shall never cease out of the land: therefore I command thee, saying, Thou shalt open thine hand wide unto thy brother, to thy poor, and to thy needy, in thy land.   DEUTERONOMY 15:11

He will regard the prayer of the destitute, and not despise their prayer.   PSALM 102:17

Blessed is he that considereth the poor: the LORD will deliver him in time of trouble. The LORD will preserve him, and keep him alive; and he shall be blessed upon the earth: and thou wilt not deliver him unto the will of his enemies.　PSALM 41:1–2

I will abundantly bless her provision: I will satisfy her poor with bread.　PSALM 132:15

Thou, O God, hast prepared of thy goodness for the poor.　PSALM 68:10

Father, let me cultivate an attitude of thankfulness for all I have. Keep me from judging or pitying those who have less and from envying those who have more. Let me be no respecter of persons, but to love all, equally, in Your name. Amen.

I start each shift with a simple prayer: "Lord, use my eyes, my ears, my heart." I could not be a nurse without my faith. I have nothing to offer but my presence. In prayerfully committing myself to God at the beginning of each shift, He gives me the comfort and love my patients need and keeps me steady in the life-and-death urgent moments.

CHAR KRAUSE, EMERGENCY DEPARTMENT RN

Ask, and it shall be given you; seek, and ye shall find; knock, and it shall be opened unto you: for every one that asketh receiveth; and he that seeketh findeth; and to him that knocketh it shall be opened.　　　MATTHEW 7:7–8

And all things, whatsoever ye shall ask in prayer, believing, ye shall receive.　　　MATTHEW 21:22

He will be very gracious unto thee at the voice of thy cry; when he shall hear it, he will answer thee.
ISAIAH 30:19

And this is the confidence that we have in him, that, if we ask any thing according to his will, he heareth us: and if we know that he hear us, whatsoever we ask, we know that we have the petitions that we desired of him.
1 JOHN 5:14–15

And it shall come to pass,

that before they call,

I will answer;

and while they are yet speaking,

I will hear.

ISAIAH 65:24

Thou shalt make thy prayer unto him, and he shall hear thee.
JOB 22:27

If ye abide in me, and my words abide in you, ye shall ask what ye will, and it shall be done unto you.
JOHN 15:7

Whatsoever ye shall ask the Father in my name, he will give it you. Hitherto have ye asked nothing in my name: ask, and ye shall receive, that your joy may be full.   JOHN 16:23–24

Confess your faults one to another, and pray one for another, that ye may be healed. The effectual fervent prayer of a righteous man availeth much.
                                        JAMES 5:16

And whatsoever ye shall ask in my name, that will I do, that the Father may be glorified in the Son. If ye shall ask any thing in my name, I will do it.
                                        JOHN 14:13–14

But thou, when thou prayest, enter into thy closet, and when thou hast shut thy door, pray to thy Father which is in secret; and thy Father which seeth in secret shall reward thee openly.   MATTHEW 6:6

He shall call upon me, and I will answer him.
                                        PSALM 91:15

The LORD is far from the wicked: but he heareth the prayer of the righteous.   PROVERBS 15:29

O thou that hearest prayer, unto thee shall all flesh come.   PSALM 65:2

But we will give ourselves continually to prayer, and to the ministry of the word.   ACTS 6:4

The righteous cry, and the LORD heareth, and delivereth them out of all their troubles.

PSALM 34:17

If ye then, being evil, know how to give good gifts unto your children, how much more shall your Father which is in heaven give good things to them that ask him?   MATTHEW 7:11

Then shalt thou call, and the LORD shall answer; thou shalt cry, and he shall say, Here I am.

ISAIAH 58:9

Pray without ceasing.

1 THESSALONIANS 5:17

Evening, and morning, and at noon, will I pray, and cry aloud: and he shall hear my voice.

PSALM 55:17

Be not ye therefore like unto them: for your Father knoweth what things ye have need of, before ye ask him.   MATTHEW 6:8

Then shall ye call upon me, and ye shall go and pray unto me, and I will hearken unto you.

JEREMIAH 29:12

The LORD is nigh unto all them that call upon him, to all that call upon him in truth. He will fulfil the desire of them that fear him: he also will hear their cry, and will save them.

PSALM 145:18–19

And whatsoever we ask, we receive of him, because we keep his commandments, and do those things that are pleasing in his sight.   1 JOHN 3:22

Give ear to my words, O LORD, consider my meditation. Hearken unto the voice of my cry, my King, and my God: for unto thee will I pray. My voice shalt thou hear in the morning, O LORD; in the morning will I direct my prayer unto thee, and will look up.   PSALM 5:1–3

Rejoicing in hope; patient in tribulation; continuing instant in prayer.   ROMANS 12:12

Praying always with all prayer and supplication in the Spirit, and watching thereunto with all perseverance and supplication for all saints.

EPHESIANS 6:18

I waited patiently for the LORD; and he inclined unto me, and heard my cry.   PSALM 40:1

Because he hath inclined his ear unto me, therefore will I call upon him as long as I live.

PSALM 116:2

If my people, which are called by my name, shall humble themselves, and pray, and seek my face, and turn from their wicked ways; then will I hear from heaven, and will forgive their sin, and will heal their land. 2 CHRONICLES 7:14

Let us therefore come boldly unto the throne of grace, that we may obtain mercy, and find grace to help in time of need. HEBREWS 4:16

The sacrifice of the wicked is an abomination to the LORD: but the prayer of the upright is his delight.
PROVERBS 15:8

Oh that men would praise

the LORD for his goodness,

and for his wonderful works

to the children of men!

PSALM 107:15

I will pray with the spirit, and I will pray with the understanding also: I will sing with the spirit, and I will sing with the understanding also.
1 CORINTHIANS 14:15

Yet the LORD will command his lovingkindness in the day time, and in the night his song shall be with me, and my prayer unto the God of my life.

PSALM 42:8

Again I say unto you, That if two of you shall agree on earth as touching any thing that they shall ask, it shall be done for them of my Father which is in heaven. For where two or three are gathered together in my name, there am I in the midst of them.

MATTHEW 18:19–20

Be careful for nothing; but in every thing by prayer and supplication with thanksgiving let your requests be made known unto God. And the peace of God, which passeth all understanding, shall keep your hearts and minds through Christ Jesus.

PHILIPPIANS 4:6–7

How sweet it is to come to You, Father. . .and how necessary. I cannot do this on my own. Knowing You are a whisper away gives me infinite comfort. Be my strength and guide today. Let me pray without ceasing—not just with my mouth, but with my heart and hands. I invite You, Lord of all, to fill me, to work in and through me, and commune with my heart to keep my soul fully, completely in tune with You. Amen.

PRIDE

The door that nobody else will go in at, seems always to swing open widely for me.

CLARA BARTON

Pride goeth before destruction, and an haughty spirit before a fall. PROVERBS 16:18

Woe unto them that are wise in their own eyes, and prudent in their own sight! ISAIAH 5:21

Seest thou a man wise in his own conceit? there is more hope of a fool than of him. PROVERBS 26:12

Let another man praise thee, and not thine own mouth; a stranger, and not thine own lips.

PROVERBS 27:2

An high look, and a proud heart, and the plowing of the wicked, is sin. PROVERBS 21:4

But he that glorieth, let him glory in the Lord. For not he that commendeth himself is approved, but whom the Lord commendeth.
2 CORINTHIANS 10:17–18

And he said unto them, Ye are they which justify yourselves before men; but God knoweth your hearts: for that which is highly esteemed among men is abomination in the sight of God.
LUKE 16:15

Thou hast rebuked the proud that are cursed, which do err from thy commandments. PSALM 119:21

How can ye believe, which receive honour one of another, and seek not the honour that cometh from God only? JOHN 5:44

And he sat down, and called the twelve, and saith unto them, If any man desire to be first, the same shall be last of all, and servant of all. MARK 9:35

Be not wise in thine own eyes: fear the LORD, and depart from evil. PROVERBS 3:7

Surely God will not hear vanity, neither will the Almighty regard it. JOB 35:13

But now ye rejoice in your boastings: all such rejoicing is evil.   JAMES 4:16

Be of the same mind one toward another. Mind not high things, but condescend to men of low estate. Be not wise in your own conceits.

ROMANS 12:16

For if a man think himself

to be something,

when he is nothing,

he deceiveth himself.

GALATIANS 6:3

Talk no more so exceeding proudly; let not arrogancy come out of your mouth: for the LORD is a God of knowledge, and by him actions are weighed.

1 SAMUEL 2:3

For I say, through the grace given unto me, to every man that is among you, not to think of himself more highly than he ought to think; but to think soberly, according as God hath dealt to every man the measure of faith.   ROMANS 12:3

When pride cometh, then cometh shame: but with
the lowly is wisdom.   PROVERBS 11:2

*I have nothing to boast about, God. All I claim is
You. Let me not think more highly of myself for any-
thing I might say and do, but let it all be to Your glory.
Amen.*

GOD'S PROTECTION

God will never leave me. He is in control, so I don't have to fear or have anxiety.

SHARON MILLER, PSYCHIATRIC RN

The name of the LORD is a strong tower: the righteous runneth into it, and is safe.

PROVERBS 18:10

You will be secure, because there is hope; you will look about you and take your rest in safety. You will lie down, with no one to make you afraid.

JOB 11:18–19 NIV

The LORD shall preserve thee from all evil: he shall preserve thy soul. The LORD shall preserve thy going out and thy coming in from this time forth, and even for evermore.

PSALM 121:7–8

And who is he that will harm you, if ye be followers of that which is good?   1 PETER 3:13

The beloved of the LORD shall dwell in safety by him; and the LORD shall cover him all the day long, and he shall dwell between his shoulders.
DEUTERONOMY 33:12

He shall not be afraid of evil tidings: his heart is fixed, trusting in the LORD.   PSALM 112:7

Because thou hast made the LORD, which is my refuge, even the most High, thy habitation; there shall no evil befall thee, neither shall any plague come nigh thy dwelling.   PSALM 91:9–10

But whoso hearkeneth unto me shall dwell safely, and shall be quiet from fear of evil.
PROVERBS 1:33

I will both lay me down in peace, and sleep: for thou, LORD, only makest me dwell in safety.
PSALM 4:8

The LORD is my light and my salvation; whom shall I fear? the LORD is the strength of my life; of whom shall I be afraid?   PSALM 27:1

In the fear of the LORD is strong confidence: and his children shall have a place of refuge. PROVERBS 14:26

When thou passest through the waters, I will be with thee; and through the rivers, they shall not overflow thee: when thou walkest through the fire, thou shalt not be burned; neither shall the flame kindle upon thee.   ISAIAH 43:2

Be thou my strong habitation, whereunto I may continually resort: thou hast given commandment to save me; for thou art my rock and my fortress.
                                                                 PSALM 71:3

But the LORD is my defence;

and my God is

the rock of my refuge.

PSALM 94:22

For thou, LORD, wilt bless the righteous; with favour wilt thou compass him as with a shield.
                                                                 PSALM 5:12

Our soul waiteth for the LORD: he is our help and our shield.   PSALM 33:20

Every word of God is pure: he is a shield unto them that put their trust in him.   PROVERBS 30:5

Thou hast also given me the shield of thy salvation: and thy right hand hath holden me up, and thy gentleness hath made me great.　　PSALM 18:35

He shall cover thee with his feathers, and under his wings shalt thou trust: his truth shall be thy shield and buckler.　　PSALM 91:4

But whoso hearkeneth unto me shall dwell safely, and shall be quiet from fear of evil.

PROVERBS 1:33

And he said, The LORD is my rock, and my fortress, and my deliverer; the God of my rock; in him will I trust: he is my shield, and the horn of my salvation, my high tower, and my refuge, my saviour; thou savest me from violence. I will call on the LORD, who is worthy to be praised: so shall I be saved from mine enemies.　　2 SAMUEL 22:2–4

Cast thy burden upon the LORD, and he shall sustain thee: he shall never suffer the righteous to be moved.　　PSALM 55:22

For thou art my rock and my fortress; therefore for thy name's sake lead me, and guide me.

PSALM 31:3

God is our refuge and strength, a very present help in trouble.　　PSALM 46:1

The eternal God is thy refuge, and underneath are
the everlasting arms.   DEUTERONOMY 33:27

The LORD also will be a refuge for the oppressed,
a refuge in times of trouble.   PSALM 9:9

*Keep me safe, Lord. In the midst of caring for oth-
ers, I need to rely on You to protect me. Be my shield
and defender. Set Your angels about me so I need not
live in fear. Amen.*

REHABILITATION

So never lose an opportunity of urging a practical beginning, however small, for it is wonderful how often in such matters the mustard-seed germinates and roots itself.

FLORENCE NIGHTINGALE

Though he fall, he shall not be utterly cast down: for the LORD upholdeth him with his hand.

PSALM 37:24

Thou shalt not curse the deaf, nor put a stumbling-block before the blind, but shalt fear thy God: I am the LORD.

LEVITICUS 19:14

Speak up for those who cannot speak for themselves; ensure justice for those who are perishing. Yes, speak up for the poor and helpless, and see that they get justice.

PROVERBS 31:8–9 NLT

Think about the many people you have taught and the weak hands you have made strong. Your words have comforted those who fell, and you have strengthened those who could not stand.

JOB 4:3–4 NCV

Therefore, strengthen the hands that are weak and the knees that are feeble.

HEBREWS 12:12 NAS

Commit your work to the Lord, then it will succeed.

PROVERBS 16:3 TLB

Be ye strong therefore, and let not your hands be weak: for your work shall be rewarded.

2 CHRONICLES 15:7

Do not fear, for I am with you; do not be dismayed, for I am your God. I will strengthen you and help you; I will uphold you with my righteous right hand. . . . For I am the LORD, your God, who takes hold of your right hand and says to you, Do not fear; I will help you.

ISAIAH 41:10, 13 NIV

After you have suffered a little while, our God, who is full of kindness through Christ, will give you his eternal glory. He personally will come and pick you up, and set you firmly in place, and make you stronger than ever. 1 PETER 5:10 TLB

Broken bodies and broken hearts, God. I look around me and see those whose lives have been shattered, and only You can put them back together. The progress is slow, unpredictable, and hard won. Help us to see each step as a victory, even the smallest skill as a triumph. Remind me this isn't just a time to master the body; it is a time to rebuild the spirit. Great and glorious Healer, You who knit each of us together in the womb, help us now as we take the unraveled threads and piece them back together.

Come alongside us in this fight. Steady us. Encourage us. Let us see the small victories as well as the great ones. Amen.

REPENTANCE

We have such an awesome God who loves us regardless of our mistakes, whatever our history may be, and despite what "baggage" we carry. We all make mistakes as God made us humans—not perfect. Asking for forgiveness from those we have wronged and seeking God's forgiveness through repentance can be very stress relieving and can begin a healthy healing process.

MARGARET K. JORDAN RN, MSN,
STUDENT CHRISTIAN NURSE FELLOWSHIP ADVISOR,
ASSISTANT PROFESSOR,
TEXAS A&M UNIVERSITY, CORPUS CHRISTI

The Lord is not slack concerning his promise, as some men count slackness; but is longsuffering to us-ward, not willing that any should perish, but that all should come to repentance.   2 PETER 3:9

If we confess our sins, he is faithful and just to forgive us our sins, and to cleanse us from all unrighteousness.   1 JOHN 1:9

The time is fulfilled, and the kingdom of God is at hand: repent ye, and believe the gospel.
MARK 1:15

The LORD is nigh unto them that are of a broken heart; and saveth such as be of a contrite spirit.
PSALM 34:18

But if the wicked will turn from all his sins that he hath committed, and keep all my statutes, and do that which is lawful and right, he shall surely live, he shall not die. All his transgressions that he hath committed, they shall not be mentioned unto him: in his righteousness that he hath done he shall live.
EZEKIEL 18:21–22

For I am not come to call the righteous, but sinners to repentance.   MATTHEW 9:13

Likewise, I say unto you, there is joy in the presence of the angels of God over one sinner that repenteth.   LUKE 15:10

Or despisest thou the riches of his goodness and forbearance and longsuffering; not knowing that the goodness of God leadeth thee to repentance?
ROMANS 2:4

He that covereth his sins shall not prosper: but whoso confesseth and forsaketh them shall have mercy.   PROVERBS 28:13

If my people, which are called by my name, shall humble themselves, and pray, and seek my face, and turn from their wicked ways; then will I hear from heaven, and will forgive their sin, and will heal their land.   2 CHRONICLES 7:14

Thou art a God ready to pardon,

gracious and merciful, slow to anger,

and of great kindness.

NEHEMIAH 9:17

For thou, Lord, art good, and ready to forgive; and plenteous in mercy unto all them that call upon thee.   PSALM 86:5

Seek ye the LORD while he may be found, call ye upon him while he is near: Let the wicked forsake his way, and the unrighteous man his thoughts: and let him return unto the LORD, and he will have mercy upon him; and to our God, for he will abundantly pardon.   ISAIAH 55:6–7

But thou, O Lord, art a God full of compassion, and gracious, longsuffering, and plenteous in mercy and truth.   PSALM 86:15

Repent ye therefore, and be converted, that your sins may be blotted out, when the times of refreshing shall come from the presence of the Lord.
ACTS 3:19

Turn unto the LORD your God: for he is gracious and merciful, slow to anger, and of great kindness, and repenteth him of the evil.   JOEL 2:13

In whom we have redemption through his blood, the forgiveness of sins, according to the riches of his grace.   EPHESIANS 1:7

Repent therefore of this thy wickedness, and pray God, if perhaps the thought of thine heart may be forgiven thee.   ACTS 8:22

Draw nigh to God, and he will draw nigh to you. Cleanse your hands, ye sinners; and purify your hearts, ye double minded.   JAMES 4:8

Come now, and let us reason together, saith the LORD: though your sins be as scarlet, they shall be white as snow; though they be red as crimson, they shall be as wool.   ISAIAH 1:18

Tender Shepherd, I kneel with a heavy heart and ask Your forgiveness. I was wrong, and nothing is more important to me than being right with You. Wash my soul free of this sin. Cleanse me and lead me in the paths of righteousness, I pray. Amen.

There is no such thing as human righteousness—we are tainted by our very nature. Christ is the only source of true righteousness. In the free gift of salvation, Christ takes upon Himself our sin and in exchange bestows upon us His perfect righteousness. As a result, we can stand before our heavenly Father without fear because He sees us clothed in the righteousness of His Son.

CAROLYN KANOW, RN, THEOLOGY STUDENT

Blessed are they which do hunger and thirst after righteousness: for they shall be filled.

MATTHEW 5:6

But seek ye first the kingdom of God, and his righteousness; and all these things shall be added unto you.　　MATTHEW 6:33

For the LORD God is a sun and shield: the LORD will give grace and glory: no good thing will he withhold from them that walk uprightly.

PSALM 84:11

For thou, LORD, wilt bless the righteous; with favour wilt thou compass him as with a shield.

PSALM 5:12

Know ye not that the unrighteous shall not inherit the kingdom of God? Be not deceived.

1 CORINTHIANS 6:9

A good man obtaineth favour of the LORD: but a man of wicked devices will he condemn.

PROVERBS 12:2

*He that trusteth in
his riches shall fall;
but the righteous shall
flourish as a branch.*

PROVERBS 11:28

So that a man shall say, Verily there is a reward for the righteous.   PSALM 58:11

Say ye to the righteous, that it shall be well with him: for they shall eat the fruit of their doings.

ISAIAH 3:10

Even a child is known by his doings, whether his work be pure, and whether it be right.

PROVERBS 20:11

Then shall thy light break forth as the morning, and thine health shall spring forth speedily: and thy righteousness shall go before thee; the glory of the LORD shall be thy rereward.   ISAIAH 58:8

Lord, who shall abide in thy tabernacle? who shall dwell in thy holy hill? He that walketh uprightly, and worketh righteousness, and speaketh the truth in his heart.   PSALM 15:1–2

Thy word is true from the beginning: and every one of thy righteous judgments endureth for ever.

PSALM 119:160

Then shall the righteous shine forth as the sun in the kingdom of their Father. Who hath ears to hear, let him hear.   MATTHEW 13:43

Light is sown for the righteous.   PSALM 97:11

The eyes of the LORD are upon the righteous, and his ears are open unto their cry.   PSALM 34:15

But know that the LORD hath set apart him that is godly for himself: the LORD will hear when I call unto him.

PSALM 4:3

The righteous cry, and the LORD heareth, and delivereth them out of all their troubles.

PSALM 34:17

Blessed are they which are persecuted for righteousness' sake: for theirs is the kingdom of heaven.

MATTHEW 5:10

He that followeth after righteousness and mercy findeth life, righteousness, and honour.

PROVERBS 21:21

The righteous shall be glad in the LORD, and shall trust in him; and all the upright in heart shall glory.

PSALM 64:10

Surely goodness and mercy shall follow me all the days of my life: and I will dwell in the house of the LORD for ever.

PSALM 23:6

Praise Your holy name for Your goodness. Bless Your name, for You have bought me at incalculable cost. Let me never forget the price paid and keep me close to You, because I cannot stand on my own. Amen.

I had the understanding that Jesus died on the cross for us and that we were all born as sinners. It never occurred to me that I had to ask to be saved. A dear woman explained it to me, led me in a prayer, and I asked to be saved. Before, salvation seemed so hard but ended up being so easy.

HEATHER WIERICHS, RN, BSN,
CARDIOTHORACIC SURGICAL

For he hath made him to be sin for us, who knew no sin; that we might be made the righteousness of God in him. 2 CORINTHIANS 5:21

I write unto you, little children, because your sins are forgiven you for his name's sake. 1 JOHN 2:12

For thus saith the LORD unto the house of Israel, Seek ye me, and ye shall live. AMOS 5:4

But if we walk in the light, as he is in the light, we have fellowship one with another, and the blood of Jesus Christ his Son cleanseth us from all sin.

1 John 1:7

Jesus answered and said unto him, Verily, verily, I say unto thee, Except a man be born again, he cannot see the kingdom of God. Nicodemus saith unto him, How can a man be born when he is old? can he enter the second time into his mother's womb, and be born? Jesus answered, Verily, verily, I say unto thee, Except a man be born of water and of the Spirit, he cannot enter into the kingdom of God. That which is born of the flesh is flesh; and that which is born of the Spirit is spirit. Marvel not that I said unto thee, Ye must be born again.

John 3:3–7

The hand of our God is upon all them for good that seek him.

Ezra 8:22

Verily, verily, I say unto you, He that heareth my word, and believeth on him that sent me, hath everlasting life, and shall not come into condemnation; but is passed from death unto life. John 5:24

For this is good and acceptable in the sight of God our Saviour; who will have all men to be saved, and to come unto the knowledge of the truth.

1 Timothy 2:3–4

The Lord is good unto them that wait for him, to the soul that seeketh him.   Lamentations 3:25

But if from thence thou shalt seek the Lord thy God, thou shalt find him, if thou seek him with all thy heart and with all thy soul.

Deuteronomy 4:29

And they that know thy name will put their trust in thee: for thou, Lord, hast not forsaken them that seek thee.   Psalm 9:10

And ye shall seek me, and find me, when ye shall search for me with all your heart.   Jeremiah 29:13

For the Lord your God is gracious and merciful, and will not turn away his face from you, if ye return unto him.   2 Chronicles 30:9

Who gave himself for our sins, that he might deliver us from this present evil world, according to the will of God and our Father.   Galatians 1:4

I, even I, am he that blotteth out thy transgressions for mine own sake, and will not remember thy sins.

Isaiah 43:25

If we confess our sins, he is faithful and just to forgive us our sins, and to cleanse us from all unrighteousness. 1 John 1:9

For I will be merciful to their unrighteousness, and their sins and their iniquities will I remember no more. Hebrews 8:12

For I will forgive their iniquity, and I will remember their sin no more. Jeremiah 31:34

As far as the east is from the west,

so far hath he removed

our transgressions from us.

Psalm 103:12

And I will cleanse them from all their iniquity, whereby they have sinned against me; and I will pardon all their iniquities, whereby they have sinned, and whereby they have transgressed against me. Jeremiah 33:8

Therefore if any man be in Christ, he is a new creature: old things are passed away; behold, all things are become new. 2 Corinthians 5:17

My little children, these things write I unto you, that ye sin not. And if any man sin, we have an advocate with the Father, Jesus Christ the righteous: and he is the propitiation for our sins: and not for ours only, but also for the sins of the whole world.
1 JOHN 2:1–2

But after that the kindness and love of God our Saviour toward man appeared, not by works of righteousness which we have done, but according to his mercy he saved us, by the washing of regeneration, and renewing of the Holy Ghost; which he shed on us abundantly through Jesus Christ our Saviour.
TITUS 3:4–6

But as many as received him, to them gave he power to become the sons of God, even to them that believe on his name: which were born, not of blood, nor of the will of the flesh, nor of the will of man, but of God.
JOHN 1:12–13

But without faith it is impossible to please him: for he that cometh to God must believe that he is, and that he is a rewarder of them that diligently seek him.
HEBREWS 11:6

Seek the LORD and his strength, seek his face continually.
1 CHRONICLES 16:11

They that seek the LORD shall not want any good thing.
PSALM 34:10

And I say unto you, Ask, and it shall be given you; seek, and ye shall find; knock, and it shall be opened unto you.   LUKE 11:9

Therefore came I forth to meet thee, diligently to seek thy face, and I have found thee.

PROVERBS 7:15

But seek ye first the kingdom of God, and his righteousness; and all these things shall be added unto you.   MATTHEW 6:33

Heavenly Father, how thankful I am for the gift of Your Son, Jesus. I cannot begin to imagine the greatness of Your love for me, that even while I was lost in my sin, You loved me so much that You sent Jesus to Calvary to die in my place.

Lord Jesus, I come to You at the cross, laying my sin bare before You, willing to accept the grace You extended to me with Your shed blood. Wash me, Lord, in Your purity and grant to me Your Holy Spirit. Amen.

I think even lying on my bed I can still do something.

DOROTHEA DIX

Is any among you afflicted? let him pray. Is any merry? let him sing psalms. Is any sick among you? let him call for the elders of the church; and let them pray over him, anointing him with oil in the name of the Lord: And the prayer of faith shall save the sick, and the Lord shall raise him up; and if he have committed sins, they shall be forgiven him.   JAMES 5:13–15

So that they cause the cry of the poor to come unto him, and he heareth the cry of the afflicted.

JOB 34:28

And when he was come into the house, the blind men came to him: and Jesus saith unto them, Believe ye that I am able to do this? They said unto him, Yea, Lord. Then touched he their eyes, saying, According to your faith be it unto you. And their eyes were opened.   MATTHEW 9:28–30

For he hath not despised nor abhorred the affliction of the afflicted; neither hath he hid his face from him; but when he cried unto him, he heard.
                                                        PSALM 22:24

For I will restore health unto thee,

and I will heal thee of thy wounds,

saith the LORD.

JEREMIAH 30:17

Who his own self bare our sins in his own body on the tree, that we, being dead to sins, should live unto righteousness: by whose stripes ye were healed.
                                                        1 PETER 2:24

For he shall give his angels charge over thee, to keep thee in all thy ways.   PSALM 91:11

Heal me, O LORD, and I shall be healed; save me, and I shall be saved: for thou art my praise.

JEREMIAH 17:14

And he said unto me, My grace is sufficient for thee: for my strength is made perfect in weakness. Most gladly therefore will I rather glory in my infirmities, that the power of Christ may rest upon me.

2 CORINTHIANS 12:9

But that ye may know that the Son of man hath power on earth to forgive sins, (then saith he to the sick of the palsy,) Arise, take up thy bed, and go unto thine house. And he arose, and departed to his house.   MATTHEW 9:6–7

Lord, we fool ourselves into thinking we can do everything on our own. How little it takes for us to remember how vulnerable and weak we are. You, alone, are strong. You, alone, are the source of all power and might, of all health and redemption. In the midst of sickness, we either reach out to You and beg for assistance or foolishly curse You. Christ cared for the soul, and physical health was secondary. Help me to tend body and soul of each of those You entrust to my care. Amen.

SPEECH

Kind words can be short and easy to speak, but their echoes are truly endless.

MOTHER TERESA

A word fitly spoken is like apples of gold in pictures of silver.   PROVERBS 25:11

Be not rash with thy mouth, and let not thine heart be hasty to utter any thing before God: for God is in heaven, and thou upon earth: therefore let thy words be few.   ECCLESIASTES 5:2

A soft answer turneth away wrath: but grievous words stir up anger.   PROVERBS 15:1

Do not lie to one another.   COLOSSIANS 3:9 NKJV

Let your speech be alway with grace, seasoned with salt, that ye may know how ye ought to answer every man.   COLOSSIANS 4:6

The heart of the wise teacheth his mouth, and addeth learning to his lips. Pleasant words are as an honeycomb, sweet to the soul, and health to the bones.   PROVERBS 16:23–24

For he that will love life, and see good days, let him refrain his tongue from evil, and his lips that they speak no guile.   1 PETER 3:10

Set a guard, O LORD,

over my mouth;

keep watch over the door of my lips.

PSALM 141:3 NKJV

Put off all these: anger, wrath, malice, blasphemy, filthy language out of your mouth.

COLOSSIANS 3:8 NKJV

A time to rend, and a time to sew; a time to keep silence, and a time to speak.   ECCLESIASTES 3:7

Let your conversation be without covetousness; and be content with such things as ye have.

HEBREWS 13:5

In the multitude of words there wanteth not sin: but he that refraineth his lips is wise.

PROVERBS 10:19

If any man offend not in word, the same is a perfect man, and able also to bridle the whole body.

JAMES 3:2

A man hath joy by the answer of his mouth: and a word spoken in due season, how good is it!

PROVERBS 15:23

The tongue of the wise useth knowledge aright: but the mouth of fools poureth out foolishness.

PROVERBS 15:2

Heavenly Father, please guard my tongue so that I do not hurt or offend anyone. Grant me the sweetness of Your love so that my speech is pleasing to You and to others. Give me words to use that will soothe and heal and mend. Amen.

I think one's feelings waste themselves in words, they ought all to be distilled into actions and into actions which bring results.

FLORENCE NIGHTINGALE

Can two walk together, except they be agreed?
AMOS 3:3

And the eye cannot say unto the hand, I have no need of thee: nor again the head to the feet, I have no need of you. 1 CORINTHIANS 12:21

Behold, how good and how pleasant it is for brethren to dwell together in unity! PSALM 133:1

Be of the same mind one toward another.
ROMANS 12:16

199

Now the God of patience and consolation grant you to be likeminded one toward another according to Christ Jesus: That ye may with one mind and one mouth glorify God, even the Father of our Lord Jesus Christ.   ROMANS 15:5–6

Finally, be ye all of one mind, having compassion one of another, love as brethren, be pitiful, be courteous. . . . Let him seek peace, and ensue it.
                                        1 PETER 3:8, 11

Now I beseech you, brethren, by the name of our Lord Jesus Christ, that ye all speak the same thing, and that there be no divisions among you; but that ye be perfectly joined together in the same mind and in the same judgment.   1 CORINTHIANS 1:10

Use hospitality one to another without grudging.
                                        1 PETER 4:9

Triune God, You who are Three-in-One, who creates the universe, gives life, and redeems souls. Here we are—a team of flesh and bone, a weary group who has so much to do and so little time to accomplish it all. Grant us Your wisdom. Organize our thoughts. Imbue us with Your love and kindness so we can work together with a caring, cooperative spirit. Amen.

R isk comes with the job of being a nurse. I deal with in-
fectious diseases, blood, dementia, psychiatric cases. . .
but I cannot live in fear. I commit myself to the Lord and
trust Him. That trust takes care of my worries so I can care
for the patients who trust me to be there for them.

CHAR KRAUSE, EMERGENCY DEPARTMENT RN

The LORD is my rock, and my fortress, and my deliverer; my God, my strength, in whom I will trust.

PSALM 18:2

God is our refuge and strength, a very present help
in trouble. Therefore will not we fear, though the
earth be removed, and though the mountains be
carried into the midst of the sea.   PSALM 46:1–2

For the LORD God is a sun and shield: the LORD will give grace and glory: no good thing will he withhold from them that walk uprightly. O LORD of hosts, blessed is the man that trusteth in thee.

PSALM 84:11–12

Trust in the Lord God always, for in the Lord Jehovah is your everlasting strength.

ISAIAH 26:4 TLB

Blessed is that man that

maketh the LORD his trust.

PSALM 40:4

Trust in the LORD, and do good; so shalt thou dwell in the land, and verily thou shalt be fed. Delight thyself also in the LORD: and he shall give thee the desires of thine heart. Commit thy way unto the LORD; trust also in him; and he shall bring it to pass.   PSALM 37:3–5

Fear not, little flock; for it is your Father's good pleasure to give you the kingdom.   LUKE 12:32

Casting all your care upon him; for he careth for you.   1 PETER 5:7

The LORD is good, a strong hold in the day of trouble; and he knoweth them that trust in him.

NAHUM 1:7

Trust in the LORD with all thine heart; and lean not unto thine own understanding. In all thy ways acknowledge him, and he shall direct thy paths.

PROVERBS 3:5–6

They that trust in the LORD shall be as mount Zion, which cannot be removed, but abideth for ever.

PSALM 125:1

Therefore take no thought, saying, What shall we eat? or, What shall we drink? or, Wherewithal shall we be clothed? (For after all these things do the Gentiles seek:) for your heavenly Father knoweth that ye have need of all these things.

MATTHEW 6:31–32

The angel of the LORD encampeth round about them that fear him, and delivereth them.

PSALM 34:7

And therefore will the LORD wait, that he may be gracious unto you, and therefore will he be exalted, that he may have mercy upon you: for the LORD is a God of judgment: blessed are all they that wait for him.

ISAIAH 30:18

But the mercy of the LORD is from everlasting to everlasting upon them that fear him, and his righteousness unto children's children.   PSALM 103:17

Father, thank You for letting me cast all my cares on You. I know You care for me as a shepherd who tends his sheep. I can rest and be calm knowing that Your hand is on me. I can trust all of Your promises, knowing that You are faithful. And I can have peace in the love You have so freely given. Great is Your faithfulness, Lord, even unto me. Amen.

I am so busy that I have not time to die.

FLORENCE NIGHTINGALE

Women never have a half-hour in all their lives (excepting before or after anybody is up in the house) that they can call their own, without fear of offending or of hurting someone. Why do people sit up so late, or, more rarely, get up so early? Not because the day is not long enough, but because they have "no time in the day to themselves."

FLORENCE NIGHTINGALE

But they that wait upon the LORD shall renew their strength; they shall mount up with wings as eagles; they shall run, and not be weary; and they shall walk, and not faint.   ISAIAH 40:31

And let us not be weary in well doing: for in due season we shall reap, if we faint not.

GALATIANS 6:9

Come unto me, all ye that labour and are heavy laden, and I will give you rest.   MATTHEW 11:28

He that dwelleth in the secret place of the most High shall abide under the shadow of the Almighty.

PSALM 91:1

Rest in the LORD, and wait patiently for him.

PSALM 37:7

I've rolled my shoulders and stretched my back. I could swim in the coffee I've had to drink so far. Jesus, You know how tired I am. I've done so much already, but even more lies ahead, yet to be done. Don't let me be like the disciples who slept while You knelt in Gethsemane—I don't want to fail You. Imbue me with Your power and refresh me with Your spirit so I can continue on. Amen.

Since the first twenty-five years of my nursing career took place in a rural setting, I was fortunate to have "download" time in the car. Frequently I used this as prayer time—my "reaching up" time. After one particularly difficult experience, I would cry on the way to work, pray, and then leave my problems with the Lord as I entered the workplace— "reaching out" to help others. Daily Bible reading—the "lamp unto my path"—enabled me to continue serving others. During prayer I expressed my anger over the unexplainable—knowing Jesus was already aware of the situation. By acknowledging my feelings, He could help me deal with them. Often He sent others to help as well—whether a patient at work, friends, a women's retreat, a song, or a particular passage of Scripture.

Favorite Scripture: "Thy word is a lamp unto my feet, and a light unto my path." Psalm 119:105

CLEDA MEYER, PH.D., RN ASSOCIATE PROFESSOR,
BAKER UNIVERSITY SCHOOL OF NURSING,
TOPEKA, KANSAS

The heart of the prudent getteth knowledge; and the ear of the wise seeketh knowledge.

PROVERBS 18:15

And wisdom and knowledge shall be the stability of thy times, and strength of salvation: the fear of the LORD is his treasure.   ISAIAH 33:6

And he will teach us of his ways, and we will walk in his paths.   ISAIAH 2:3

For the LORD giveth wisdom:

out of his mouth cometh

knowledge and understanding.

PROVERBS 2:6

Now therefore hearken unto me, O ye children: for blessed are they that keep my ways. Hear instruction, and be wise, and refuse it not.

PROVERBS 8:32–33

For God giveth to a man that is good in his sight wisdom, and knowledge, and joy.

ECCLESIASTES 2:26

Teach me good judgment and knowledge: for I have believed thy commandments.   PSALM 119:66

I will bless the LORD, who hath given me counsel: my reins also instruct me in the night seasons.
PSALM 16:7

Behold, thou desirest truth in the inward parts: and in the hidden part thou shalt make me to know wisdom.   PSALM 51:6

A wise man's heart discerneth both time and judgment.   ECCLESIASTES 8:5

Say unto wisdom, Thou art my sister; and call understanding thy kinswoman.   PROVERBS 7:4

Wherefore be ye not unwise, but understanding what the will of the LORD is.   EPHESIANS 5:17

Therefore whosoever heareth these sayings of mine, and doeth them, I will liken him unto a wise man, which built his house upon a rock: and the rain descended, and the floods came, and the winds blew, and beat upon that house; and it fell not: for it was founded upon a rock.   MATTHEW 7:24–25

He that is void of wisdom despiseth his neighbour: but a man of understanding holdeth his peace.
PROVERBS 11:12

The LORD by wisdom hath founded the earth; by understanding hath he established the heavens. By his knowledge the depths are broken up, and the clouds drop down the dew. My son, let not them depart from thine eyes: keep sound wisdom and discretion.   PROVERBS 3:19–21

A prudent man concealeth knowledge: but the heart of fools proclaimeth foolishness.

PROVERBS 12:23

Whoso is wise,

and will observe these things,

even they shall understand the

lovingkindness of the LORD.

PSALM 107:43

And unto man he said, Behold, the fear of the LORD, that is wisdom; and to depart from evil is understanding.   JOB 28:28

How much better is it to get wisdom than gold! and to get understanding rather to be chosen than silver!   PROVERBS 16:16

And they that be wise shall shine as the brightness
of the firmament; and they that turn many to righteousness as the stars for ever and ever.

DANIEL 12:3

He that handleth a matter wisely shall find good:
and whoso trusteth in the LORD, happy is he. The
wise in heart shall be called prudent: and the
sweetness of the lips increaseth learning.

PROVERBS 16:20–21

Who is wise, and he shall understand these things?
prudent, and he shall know them? for the ways of
the LORD are right, and the just shall walk in them:
but the transgressors shall fall therein.

HOSEA 14:9

My son, attend to my words; incline thine ear unto
my sayings. Let them not depart from thine eyes;
keep them in the midst of thine heart. For they are
life unto those that find them, and health to all
their flesh.   PROVERBS 4:20–22

I will instruct thee and teach thee in the way which
thou shalt go: I will guide thee with mine eye.

PSALM 32:8

If any of you lack wisdom, let him ask of God, that
giveth to all men liberally, and upbraideth not; and
it shall be given him.   JAMES 1:5

My son, eat thou honey, because it is good; and the honeycomb, which is sweet to thy taste: so shall the knowledge of wisdom be unto thy soul: when thou hast found it, then there shall be a reward, and thy expectation shall not be cut off.

PROVERBS 24:13–14

The simple believeth every word: but the prudent man looketh well to his going.　PROVERBS 14:15

And if any man think that he knoweth any thing, he knoweth nothing yet as he ought to know.

1 CORINTHIANS 8:2

For wisdom is a defence, and money is a defence: but the excellency of knowledge is, that wisdom giveth life to them that have it.　ECCLESIASTES 7:12

Father, I pray for wisdom in all I do today. All of the knowledge of man is foolishness to You. Help me to rely on You, to seek Your face, to follow Your will. Grant me clarity of thought, purity of purpose, and the strength to complete all that needs to be accomplished. Amen.

A man usually values that most for which he has labored; he uses that most frugally which he has toiled hour by hour and day by day to acquire.

DOROTHEA DIX

*P*aul modeled how we are to strive on at the work God assigns us. Salvation is free, but our walk with the Lord is manifested in the work we do. The prize isn't ours until the work is done—to show God's grace and mercy to our patients. We come away successful because of what His love does in our hearts and through our hands.

DR. MICHELE CHEYLETTE,
CHAIR OF THE DEPARTMENT OF NURSING,
LOUISIANA COLLEGE

For thou shalt eat the labour of thine hands: happy shalt thou be, and it shall be well with thee.

PSALM 128:2

And also that every man should eat and drink, and enjoy the good of all his labour, it is the gift of God.

ECCLESIASTES 3:13

The LORD shall open unto thee his good treasure, the heaven to give the rain unto thy land in his season, and to bless all the work of thine hand: and thou shalt lend unto many nations, and thou shalt not borrow.

DEUTERONOMY 28:12

Be ye strong therefore,

and let not your hands be weak:

for your work shall be rewarded.

2 CHRONICLES 15:7

Even a child is known by his doings, whether his work be pure, and whether it be right.

PROVERBS 20:11

Not slothful in business; fervent in spirit; serving the Lord.

ROMANS 12:11

Then said they unto him, What shall we do, that we might work the works of God? Jesus answered and said unto them, This is the work of God, that ye believe on him whom he hath sent.

JOHN 6: 28–29

Therefore, my beloved brethren, be ye stedfast, unmoveable, always abounding in the work of the Lord, forasmuch as ye know that your labour is not in vain in the Lord.   1 CORINTHIANS 15:58

Every man also to whom God hath given riches and wealth, and hath given him power to eat thereof, and to take his portion, and to rejoice in his labour; this is the gift of God.   ECCLESIASTES 5:19

That ye might walk worthy of the Lord unto all pleasing, being fruitful in every good work, and increasing in the knowledge of God.

COLOSSIANS 1:10

For we hear that there are some which walk among you disorderly, working not at all, but are busybodies. Now them that are such we command and exhort by our Lord Jesus Christ, that with quietness they work, and eat their own bread.

2 THESSALONIANS 3:11–12

Except the LORD build the house, they labour in vain that build it: except the LORD keep the city, the watchman waketh but in vain.   PSALM 127:1

For God is not unrighteous to forget your work and labour of love, which ye have shewed toward his name, in that ye have ministered to the saints, and do minister. And we desire that every one of you do shew the same diligence to the full assurance of hope unto the end.   HEBREWS 6:10–11

In all labour there is profit: but the talk of the lips tendeth only to penury.   PROVERBS 14:23

Let him that stole steal no more: but rather let him labour, working with his hands the thing which is good, that he may have to give to him that needeth.
                    EPHESIANS 4:28

I've tied on my shoes and washed my hands, Lord. I'm ready to take on my assignment. Whatever this shift holds, let me do all to Your glory. Fill me with patience and kindness, and squeeze in an extra moment for me to give each patient a tender word and touch in Your name. Grant me the endurance to shoulder the physical challenges and the clarity to use my skills to their utmost advantage. At the end of each day, I want to hear Your praise, "Well done, good and faithful servant." Amen.

N *ever worry about numbers. Help one person at a time,*
and always start with the person nearest you.

MOTHER TERESA

Be careful for nothing; but in every thing by prayer
and supplication with thanksgiving let your requests be made known unto God. And the peace
of God, which passeth all understanding, shall
keep your hearts and minds through Christ Jesus.

PHILIPPIANS 4:6–7

God is our refuge and strength, a very present help
in trouble. Therefore will not we fear, though the
earth be removed, and though the mountains be
carried into the midst of the sea; though the waters
thereof roar and be troubled, though the mountains
shake with the swelling thereof.   PSALM 46:1–3

217

For he shall be as a tree planted by the waters, and that spreadeth out her roots by the river, and shall not see when heat cometh, but her leaf shall be green; and shall not be careful in the year of drought, neither shall cease from yielding fruit.

JEREMIAH 17:8

But my God shall supply

all your need according to

his riches in glory

by Christ Jesus.

PHILIPPIANS 4:19

Thou art my hiding place; thou shalt preserve me from trouble; thou shalt compass me about with songs of deliverance.   PSALM 32:7

He shall call upon me, and I will answer him: I will be with him in trouble; I will deliver him, and honour him.   PSALM 91:15

We are troubled on every side, yet not distressed; we are perplexed, but not in despair; Persecuted, but not forsaken; cast down, but not destroyed.

2 CORINTHIANS 4:8–9

And we know that all things work together for good to them that love God, to them who are the called according to his purpose. ROMANS 8:28

And the work of righteousness shall be peace; and the effect of righteousness quietness and assurance for ever. ISAIAH 32:17

Nursing pulls on my soul, Lord. You know what I've seen today. Did I do everything I could? Did I remember all of the details? Was there some other way I could have given comfort to the family burdened by such a heavy load? There are days when I'm sure I'm growing old far before my time, carrying the concerns I do. You invite me to take Your yoke upon me, to lean upon Your strength and wisdom. Lift the weight from my heart, Jesus. Walk beside me and remind me that You are in control. Amen.

WORSHIP

Worship is where I top off my cup of joy. I'm able to kneel in the presence of God and be thankful for His wisdom, knowledge, and foresight. He is faithful in the obvious and not-so-obvious things, even when I am shortsighted.

TRACEY LARSON, RN

All the earth shall worship thee, and shall sing unto thee; they shall sing to thy name.   PSALM 66:4

O come, let us worship and bow down: let us kneel before the LORD our maker. For he is our God; and we are the people of his pasture, and the sheep of his hand.   PSALM 95:6–7

The LORD liveth; and blessed be my rock; and exalted be the God of the rock of my salvation.

2 SAMUEL 22:47

I will praise the LORD according to his righteousness: and will sing praise to the name of the LORD most high.   PSALM 7:17

The four and twenty elders fall down before him that sat on the throne, and worship him that liveth for ever and ever, and cast their crowns before the throne, saying, Thou art worthy, O Lord, to receive glory and honour and power: for thou hast created all things, and for thy pleasure they are and were created.   REVELATION 4:10–11

By the breath of God ice is given, and the broad waters are frozen. . . . Stand still and consider the wondrous works of God.   JOB 37:10, 14 NKJV

All nations whom thou hast made shall come and worship before thee, O Lord; and shall glorify thy name.   PSALM 86:9

Who shall not fear thee, O Lord, and glorify thy name? for thou only art holy: for all nations shall come and worship before thee; for thy judgments are made manifest.   REVELATION 15:4

And I fell at his feet to worship him. And he said unto me, See thou do it not: I am thy fellowservant, and of thy brethren that have the testimony of Jesus: worship God: for the testimony of Jesus is the spirit of prophecy.   REVELATION 19:10

Exalt the LORD our God, and worship at his holy hill; for the LORD our God is holy.   PSALM 99:9

And the devil said unto him, All this power will I give thee, and the glory of them: for that is delivered unto me; and to whomsoever I will I give it. If thou therefore wilt worship me, all shall be thine. And Jesus answered and said unto him, Get thee behind me, Satan: for it is written, Thou shalt worship the Lord thy God, and him only shalt thou serve.

LUKE 4:6–8

God is a Spirit:

and they that worship him

must worship him in spirit

and in truth.

JOHN 4:24

And the four and twenty elders, which sat before God on their seats, fell upon their faces, and worshipped God, saying, We give thee thanks, O LORD God Almighty, which art, and wast, and art to come; because thou hast taken to thee thy great power, and hast reigned.   REVELATION 11:16–17

Omnipotent, Almighty God, You created mankind, but You also form each individual. I kneel in awe of Your power and might; I sing praise for Your workmanship. How wonderful it is for me to slip my hand into Yours, to be of service to those who need compassion and care. Thank You for being the wellspring of knowledge and wisdom, of health, strength, and mercy. It is an honor to be Your vessel, Your hands, Your servant as I care for my patients. Amen.

THE FLORENCE NIGHTINGALE PLEDGE

I solemnly pledge myself before God and presence of this assembly; to pass my life in purity and to practice my profession faithfully.

I will abstain from whatever is deleterious and mischievous and will not take or knowingly administer any harmful drug.

I will do all in my power to maintain and elevate the standard of my profession and will hold in confidence all personal matters committed to my keeping and family affairs coming to my knowledge in the practice of my calling.

With loyalty will I endeavor to aid the physician in his work and devote myself to the welfare of those committed to my care.

Be joyful in hope, patient in affliction, faithful in prayer.
ROMANS 12:12 NIV